ENTRY POINTS:

A Guide to Rudolf Steiner's
Study of Man

ENTRY POINTS

A Guide to Rudolf Steiner's
Study of Man

EDITED BY
ELAN LEIBNER

Waldorf
PUBLICATIONS
RESEARCH INSTITUTE FOR *Waldorf* EDUCATION

Printed with support from the Waldorf Curriculum Fund

Printed by:

Waldorf Publications at the
Research Institute for Waldorf Education
38 Main Street
Chatham, NY 12037

Title: *Entry Points: A Guide to Rudolf Steiner's* Study of Man
Editor: Elan Leibner
Layout: Ann Erwin
Proofreaders: Ruth Riegel
Cover image: *Silver Thread*, painting by Ursula Stone

Table of Contents

Introduction

As Waldorf education nears the 100th anniversary of its founding, the leadership of the Pedagogical Section of the School for Spiritual Science in Dornach, Switzerland, is suggesting that three themes be taken up by every school across the world:

~ study of the foundational opening lectures of the original teachers' preparation course (*Study of Man*, also known as *The Foundations of Human Experience*),

~ child study, and

~ beekeeping.

This is a threefold approach: One suggestion is for the teacher's inner and professional development, one focuses on the healthy development of students, and one is a form of caring for nature and the world around the school.

The Pedagogical Section Council of North America (PSC) decided to support this initiative through the creation and distribution of this book. It is meant to assist in a deeper understanding and appreciation of Rudolf Steiner's lecture cycle to the first circle of Waldorf teachers. The Council's collective experience is that, because the text is demanding and lengthy, faculties have difficulty working through the entire cycle and, instead, drop it somewhere along the way. With this objective in mind, we have resolved to create a book that will:

~ present an overview of the content of these 14 lectures,

~ address certain thorny questions,

~ suggest questions for entry into discussion, and

~ add commentaries on a few selected topics.

For each lecture there are four contributions: a summary of the lecture with footnotes, commentary by Betty Staley, and study questions for guiding discussions.

The purpose of the summaries is to help the reader maintain an overview of the whole lecture cycle. A summary is no substitute for a careful reading of the text, but it can act like a floor plan to a cathedral or a museum: It will keep one from losing orientation in the vastness of the edifice. The summaries can also be read one after another, giving the reader a bird's-eye view of how a section of the book progresses and builds a coherent whole.

As Steiner mentions repeatedly, this lecture cycle is essentially divided into three parts following an introductory first lecture:

~ Lectures 2–5 look at the human being from the point of view of the *soul*.

~ Lectures 6–9 examine the human being from the point of view of the *spirit*.

~ Lectures 10–14 take up a detailed study of the human being from the point of view of the *body*.

The summaries of a whole section can be read consecutively, in order to gain an orientation for the perspective of the entire section as Steiner develops it.

The footnotes provided by Michael Holdrege address topics that require specialized knowledge. These typically concern fields that are not within the expertise of most teachers.

Betty Staley's commentaries stem from her concern that some of Rudolf Steiner's statements continue to be read uncritically or outside the context of developments since his time. A hundred years on, humanity has learned a few things in psychology and medicine, for example, and Staley adds a perspective born of her fifty-plus years as a Waldorf educator.

The questions for guiding discussion and study are offered by David Weber and, apart from inviting individual readers to ponder them, can help the facilitators of a faculty study steer the conversation.

Our experience in Pedagogical Section conferences has been that following the summaries with artistic work is a wonderful way to proceed. The summaries can be divided into sections by themes, and the group can engage with the sequence of themes utilizing one or more artistic modalities (e.g., pastels, movement, poetry writing). A large group can also divide into two or more subgroups, each approaching the content through a different art, and then share the work. Artistic engagement involves feeling and will, as well as thinking, and people tend to enter more deeply into the study when the totality of their souls is involved. At the end of the booklet there are samples from the PSC's study of Lecture 6.

The intention of this book is to make it useful as a guide to the study. Teachers are exceedingly busy and often feel a certain degree of guilt about the things they are not doing. The last thing we want to do is add another text to the list of unread volumes sitting on the bookshelves of hapless teachers. We hope that this text can help its readers find Steiner's lectures more accessible and engaging.

– Elan Leibner
For the Pedagogical Section Council
April 2017

Introductory Lecture
August 21, 1919

The Waldorf School should revolutionize the educational system, which in turn is at the heart of the spiritual question of the time. This spiritual question is the foundation of the entire social organism. The teachers thus have a heavy responsibility to assure the success of the school. This success will prove the effectiveness of anthroposophy.

The school will only consider how to teach in a manner demanded by the totality of the human being. However, compromises with the political state will be necessary. The educational goals of the state are the worst imaginable, treating people like pawns or cogs in a wheel. Bolshevik schools are an example of the "progress" being made—they are the grave of all true teaching. Nevertheless, the cultural deed of the Waldorf School must be done.

The school's ideals and the surrounding reality must be brought into harmony; this will require everyone's full strength and effort. Therefore, the school will be organized like a republic of teachers, without a higher up (school board) to give directives. It is the pedagogy that should unify the school.

(Steiner then gives an explanation of the structure of the course.)

The Waldorf School is not parochial. It is not teaching anthroposophy, but rather using anthroposophy to develop teaching methods. The (required) religious instruction will be given according to the child's family's denomination.

The teachers must have a lively interest in everything happening in the world. They must bring enthusiasm, flexibility of spirit and devotion to their task.

Commentary

In 1919 Rudolf Steiner presented *Study of Man* (14 lectures) to the future teachers of the first Waldorf school. Because they were already deeply connected with anthroposophy, Steiner did not have to further develop his statements. However, his assumptions at that time pose challenges for readers today when we teach or discuss *Study of Man* in teacher education courses, faculty workshops, or conferences. The readers may be new to anthroposophy or they may have only a brief understanding of child development from the Waldorf perspective. In addition, times have changed. A great deal of research has occurred in neuroscience, and psychology has broadened to include views from a spiritual and soul perspective. Although this research and view may not be from an anthroposophical perspective, participants are more open to such considerations than they were in the early 20th century. Were Rudolf Steiner alive today, he might have spoken in a different way.

Much of what Steiner has expressed in these lectures is difficult. Some ideas have to be taken in and meditated upon even to gain a glimmer of grasping the complexity arising from his research. All of this poses a challenge to those who are leading discussions or studies of this fundamental work. Anthroposophy is based on freedom. Students should be able to question, agree, disagree, or take the statements as a hypothesis. It does not help if students or teachers imitate Steiner's statements without understanding them, as this leads to dogmatism.

On the other hand, there are very helpful, practical comments in each chapter of *Study of Man* that can guide teachers in their understanding of child development and Waldorf pedagogy. These provide an opportunity for students to connect with these thoughts in a way that allows for deeper reflection over time.

I have examined each lecture and found significant thoughts that I feel are accessible and useful. I am sure many Waldorf educators can add depth and breadth to my comments, but I offer these as a starting point.

Lecture 1
August 21, 1919

The work will be possible only if it is seen not just as a matter of intellect and feeling, but as a moral, spiritual task. Therefore, right from the beginning, the connection with the spiritual beings that stand behind the work will be contemplated.

(College Imagination)

The founding of the school is an event, a ceremony within the Cosmic Order. On the physical plane, Mr. Molt has to be thanked for making the moment possible. The coming together of all involved is a karmic moment, so that the festive Cosmic Moment can occur.

(Mr. Molt vows to do what he can.)

Our educational task is specific to the fifth post-Atlantean era. It is not an education for all times. Each age has its tasks. Materialism has estranged people from the specificity of historical contexts.

The children you will receive will bring with them the results of the upbringing (or the neglect) of their parents, and we will have to correct for much of what is done at home.

This neglect is connected to the self-interest, the egotism that predominates modern consciousness—an example of which is the focus on life after death but not before birth. We must be aware that before birth the child was in the spiritual world, guided by spiritual beings, until conditions were such that she had to take on a physical/etheric constitution. Thus, when we receive the child, we are continuing the work of spiritual beings.

People today think abstractly, and so it is that questions are raised about prenatal education. But before birth, the child is in the care of spiritual beings. What the parents, and especially the mother, should do is concentrate on leading a moral life. That self-education effort will yield results that will transfer to the child. Education only begins when the child breathes physical air.

Before birth, the three spirit members unite with the three soul members (Spirit Human, Life Spirit and Spirit Self unite with Consciousness Soul, Comprehension Soul and Sentient Soul). These spirit/soul members unite with a second pair of united triads: The physical body, etheric body and astral body unite with the three kingdoms of nature (mineral, plant and animal). The lower united trinity is the temporal body. Those two trinities are not at first harmonized, and our task is to support their harmonization.

Specifically, this task is to be accomplished by first under-standing the importance of breathing—the most important relationship of the human being to the physical world. Breathing connects to the metabolism through blood circulation, and to the nerve-sense pole through pressing the cerebrospinal fluid into (inbreathing) and out of the brain.[1]

In children, the breathing does not yet properly support the nerve-sense process. By teaching them how to breathe properly, we draw the spirit-soul into the physical (upper trinity into the lower).

Also, children cannot yet sleep in a manner appropriate to life on earth. They cannot process the events of waking life during sleep. We cannot give them anything from the higher worlds—that is the role of higher beings during sleep—but if we teach properly, they can take the substance of the day into sleep, and then it can flow back to them in the morning as strength.

All teaching is about proper breathing and the rhythm between sleeping and waking. Though these will not be addressed directly, everything will either bring the spirit/soul into the temporal (breathing) or the temporal into the spirit/soul (sleeping).

This is important because the teachers must focus not just on what they do, but on what they are. By having the correct thoughts about human development, the teachers can quell what is mere personality within them and become effective in a much deeper sense. By having these cosmic thoughts, over time you will create the right relationship with the students. Superficial occurrences such as rascally behavior will not bother you; you will think of it like getting caught in a rain shower without an umbrella: not pleasant, but not a serious problem, either.

The cultivation of the right thoughts will, in time, allow us to develop the right relationships with the students. We must make something of ourselves so that a living, inner spiritual relationship exists between the teacher and the children. We must remember that they came to earth to accomplish what cannot be accomplished in the spiritual world, namely an integration of the temporal and the spiritual through breathing and the rhythmic alternation between sleeping and waking. Though we will obviously not teach these two directly, they should *"guide us as a thought concerning the essence of the human being."*

Endnote

1   **Cerebrospinal fluid (CSF):** Studied extensively in the 19th century, the relationship between respiratory rhythms and the pulsation of cerebrospinal fluid (CSF) was part of the basic knowledge of medicine when these lectures were given. CSF is produced in the brain ventricles and flows outward through three openings into a CSF-filled space (subarachnoid space) surrounding the brain. The brain floats in this fluid-filled space so that its weight is reduced from around 1300 grams to 30 grams.

The spinal cord also floats in this fluid. The space around the spinal canal contains a network of veins embedded in semifluid fat. During inhalation, pressure is put on the abdominal cavity, which forces blood out of that region into the veins around the spinal canal. The swelling of the veins presses the CSF up into the brain area above. With every outbreath the pressure is released and the fluid descends again. The rhythmic pulsing of the CSF that results not only encircles the brain but, through fine pores, also penetrates into the gray matter of the cerebral cortex. This breathing-dependent movement of the CSF can be observed in the large fontanel of infants: When a baby cries the fontanel bulges. When, for diagnostic reasons, a lumbar puncture must be performed on a crying infant, pressurized fluid spurts out from the puncture needle in a high arc with every cry!

It has also been determined that CSF pressure increases when more difficult arithmetic problems are assigned. The reader can also observe what happens to her/his breathing when she solves a mental math problem such as 13 x 18. When thought activity intensifies, breathing slows down or is interrupted.

Resources: Husemann (2013); Constanzo (2013); Kranich (2003); Rohen (2001); Benninghoff-Goerttler (1977)

Commentary: Epoch of the Consciousness Soul

At the beginning of the first lecture, Rudolf Steiner mentions that each epoch has its own particular tasks. The epoch in which we live, which began in the 15th century, is referred to as the Consciousness Soul age, a time beginning with the Renaissance and focused on individualism and self-awareness. We can call this a time of modernity in which a global consciousness and freedom are awakening.

Steiner sets the tone for the teacher's attitude toward childhood—one of reverence toward all that the child brings from the past. Through our education, we have to carry on what was done by higher beings without our participation. Whether or not we consider the spiritual world real, contemplating such a possibility awakens an attitude toward the child that opens up many possibilities. This tone of reverence continues throughout the lectures so that we can sense that *Study of Man* is no ordinary teacher training manual, but a window into something beyond our everyday understanding.

Steiner highlights that the moral quality of the mother as she carries the child *in utero* passes over to the child. Current research supports this statement that the mother's attitude during the prenatal time, surrounding the incoming child with love and support, makes a great difference in a child's life.

In this lecture Rudolf Steiner describes that the task of education in the spiritual sense is to bring the Soul-Spirit into harmony with the Life Body. He introduces the terms *sentient* or *astral body*, *etheric body* and *physical body*. Gaining a background in what these terms mean is an essential part of early Waldorf teacher education and needs to be revisited over and over again. Working with these subtle bodies is a bedrock of the Waldorf teacher's understanding of human development, which will evolve over time. Without a basic knowledge of these terms, the rest of the lectures will be difficult to understand, even superficially. A helpful introduction is given in *The Education of the Child in the Light of Anthroposophy*. One can go deeper with *Theosophy* or *An Outline of Esoteric Science*, chapter 2.

Rudolf Steiner gives the teacher two goals: to pay attention to all that rightly organizes the breathing process into the nerve-sense process and to guide the children so that they can have healthy sleep. By harmonizing the breathing process with the nerve-sense process, the teacher is drawing soul and spirit into the physical life of the child. With experience, we sense how times of contraction and times of expansion bring healthy rhythm into our lessons. Over time we become more conscious of what it feels like in the classroom when this harmonizing process is happening.

Based on Steiner's description of the child's sleeping experience wherein he is in contact with the spiritual world, we can begin to sense what we bring to the child, which he can give over to the spiritual world when he is sleeping, and what he brings back from the spiritual world.

Due to the frenetic pace of life today, many children have breathing problems and sleeping problems. Waldorf teachers can bring health to the children through understanding these two processes and taking up Steiner's two challenges.

Steiner addresses the curriculum. Every subject is working toward bringing either more Spirit-Soul into the earthly body or more bodily nature into the Spirit-Soul. Here he only alludes to the subjects that pull the children out of themselves and those that ground the children in their earthly consciousness. In other lectures he describes this more fully.

The last part of Lecture 1 focuses on the teacher. If teachers take themselves seriously and work with the thoughts of the evolving human being, they will carry an inner quality that creates a warm relationship with their students. Steiner sounds the call for teachers to work on inner development so that they affect children not so much by what they know, but by who they are.

Study Questions

1. Rudolf Steiner says that the breathing connects to the whole organism in the child when she is born. In what ways does breathing affect the threefold human being?
2. Give five examples of "soul breathing" that connect the child to the physical world.
3. What does it mean to bring the physical world into the child's spirit?
4. What kinds of specific activities in the classroom help the child harmonize the breathing?
5. How is forgetting and remembering a kind of breathing?
6. What does it mean for the child to carry the impressions of the day into the spiritual world at night?
7. How can we work in the classroom to support the child's proper sleeping?
8. What does it mean for the teacher to have a strong ego, but not be self-centered or egotistical?
9. How can we develop these qualities (in Q8 above)?
10. How would you describe the process of a child's incarnation of the soul-spirit into the life-body to parents?
11. Comment on your experience of healthy "soul breathing" within a lesson. What kind of sensitivity or attunement is required of the teacher to bring this about?
12. Give examples of soul breathing for the children that we as teachers can work with consciously in: a lesson, a day, a week, a month, a year.

13. What might be wrong with a goal of maintaining perfect order in the classroom at all times?

14. Is it possible to do a little rückshau with children at the end of the school day? Could it be helpful? How might you do it?

15. How do you as a teacher work with the night in relation to your students and your lessons?

16. How do you work with memory in your daily review with the children?

Lecture 2
August 22, 1919

Pedagogy needs to develop on the basis of a psychology founded upon anthroposophy. Modern psychology is devoid of true content; its concepts are a mere playing with words. It has, for example, no real understanding of thinking or will.[2] Due to a historical necessity, there is no understanding of the connection of the individual human soul with the cosmos, but in order to understand human nature you must gain an idea of this relationship.

Anyone contemplating thoughts will be struck by their pictorial nature. Thoughts are not existential features like the physical body's parts; the latter (eyes, stomach, etc.) are real, but we cannot think with them. Thoughts are, in contrast, pictures that allow us to know things. They do not exist in themselves. Not *cogito ergo sum*, because in "cogito" there is only "non sum." "*As far as my cognition is concerned, I do not exist; only a picture exists.*"

The mobility of thoughts, as we observe them, gives us an inadequate conception of an activity, which nevertheless resonates with existence. The pictorial nature of thoughts means that our cognitive conceptions are metamorphoses of pictures. Noticing the pictorial nature of thoughts, we must inquire after the origin of the picture—just like a mirror has to reflect something, so do thoughts. What they reflect is our life before birth. [Our understanding of things goes back to our being one with them. – EL]

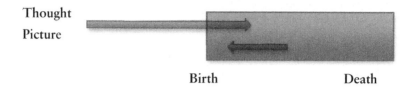

Pictorially speaking, during the course of life between birth and death, the activity from life before birth is reflected by human nature in the form of pictorial thinking. Thinking reflects pre-birth existence.

The will is baffling to psychologists because it does not seem to have any content—it is activity. In reality the will is the seed within us of what our soul-spiritual reality will be after death. In the picture above, we can add an arrow beginning within life, but extending past death. [A second picture was drawn with both arrows – EL] In this sense it is super-real, because its full reality will come about only after death. Thinking's picture nature is sub-real, in contrast, because its full reality has already passed.

So human soul life lies between the pictorial, sub-real thinking and the seed-like, super-real willing. What forces are active here? Something must reflect pre-birth reality and inhibit the germination of post-death reality: antipathy and sympathy.

We incarnate because we can no longer stay in the spiritual world; therefore we develop an antipathy towards it, causing its reality to become a mere picture. Conversely, we have sympathy towards our future return to the spirit world, which manifests itself in the will. We are not directly conscious of these two forces.

"They represent our feeling, which is a continuous interplay between sympathy and antipathy."

The rhythmic alternation between sympathy and antipathy, between ideas and will, creates the germinal soul life of the human being, the experience of feeling.

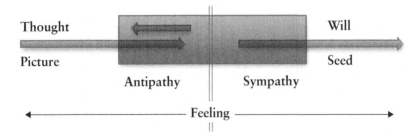

The living reality of mutual knowing (cognition) with spiritual beings in the spirit world before birth is reduced to pictures (in thoughts) through antipathy. If the antipathy is strong enough, then memory arises. Memory can only come about because we separate enough from our thoughts (through antipathy), developing a kind of disgust for them, so that they are reflected in our consciousness. When we picture something, reflect it in memory, and retain the picture, then concepts are created.

Willing is the opposite—we have sympathy for the [post-death] seed element, and heightened sympathy begets imagination. If the imaginations are strong enough, then the ordinary pictures of the things around us arise. Psychologists are wrong who think that we arrive at concepts by observing things and abstracting from them. The perception of a chalk as white arises out of the use of the will in the senses, while the concept arises out of memory.[3]

We cannot grasp human nature without understanding the soul as the interplay of sympathy and antipathy. These soul forces are seen in their full reality in the spirit world only after death.

These soul forces find expression in the temporal body as follows. The antipathy force, memory and concepts fashion the nervous system; this pole organizes the nervous system during prenatal existence. On the other side, sympathy, imagination and living pictures, all possessing a seed-like nature, create a substance that has a continual tendency to become spiritual: the blood. This tendency is arrested by our egotistical love for it; we keep it in ourselves as blood, but of itself it would dissolve into spirit. It is the temporal counterpart to the nerves, just as sympathy is the counterpart to antipathy.

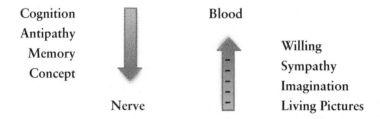

Cognition
Antipathy
Memory
Concept

Nerve

Blood

Willing
Sympathy
Imagination
Living Pictures

Blood is created and destroyed all the time through inhaling and exhaling.[4] We destroy its desire to whirl up as a vortex of spirit, turning it into a substance we can keep on earth.

The physical polarity of blood and nerves is that, whereas blood always wants to become more spiritual, the nerves would die continuously; they are made of excreted material, pointing towards matter.[5]

We will see how these principles can help us shape instruction so that it leads to soundness of mind and body. Faulty concepts are the cause of much failure in education. For example, the notion of "motor nerves" is nonsense. In reality, the so-called motor nerves allow us perception (consciousness) of our limbs. No consciousness, no movement. Our age has become lost in conceptual errors, and this gives us the opportunity to work through these errors towards human freedom.[6]

Thus it is shown how the human being and the cosmos are linked: Our pre-birth, cosmic existence finds expression in the reflective nature of thoughts, while our future cosmic existence finds expression, seed-like, in the will.

There are three places in the body where sympathy and antipathy play into one another: in the head (in the interplay of blood and nerves in the brain), in the spinal column where one nerve enters posteriorly and another exits anteriorly in each vertebra, and in the limbs where the ganglia develop into the sympathetic nerves. In each of those cases there is a gap in the nervous pathways, and a spark jumps from one nerve to the next.[7] That is where the soul connects with the body, where sympathy and antipathy enter the temporal realm.

So as we develop activities that are to continue in the cosmos, the cosmos unfolds activities in us. Both sympathy and antipathy have aspects that we develop and aspects that the cosmos develops together with us.

Physically, we appear divided into three regions: the head, the chest and the limbs (with which the metabolism is connected). Those who would want a more differentiated division, and also would want to delineate each section with strong boundaries, will attack this division. But in reality a stronger distinction is not possible. Each of these regions is only the clearest case of its own gesture, but includes the other two as well. The head, for example, is the main seat of the sense organs, but inasmuch as we sense touch and temperature throughout the body, we are "head" everywhere. And so it is with the other regions, albeit not as obvious with the limbs as pedants would like it to be. The abdomen is similarly the main location of digestion, but we have digestive processes in the brain also, and in fact our ability to feed the inner parts of the brain through the digestive processes of the outer mantle is what allows our brain the possibility of expressing (mirroring) the higher cognitive faculties of our soul.[8]

Why do we have the polarity of head and limbs-abdomen? The cosmos rejects, or, so to speak, expels the human being, and the head is the image of the cosmos from whence we are expelled. It is a picture of cosmic antipathy. Within this head, pictures of the cosmos appear, and their nature [their non-being] allows us to develop freedom. In contrast, the cosmos is sympathetic towards our limbs and the sexual organs connected with them. They beget the future in mutual sympathy with the cosmos, whereas our perceptions arise in a collision of antipathies between the cosmos and us.

Seeing this relationship between the human being and the cosmos right into the temporal body, we can understand that there is a tremendous difference between educating children rationally, conceptually, and developing their will. Emphasis on conceptual instruction actually injures the children, because it focuses on what they have already completed before birth. We must bring more pictures instead, developing our instruction out of sympathy and imagination. Overly conceptual teaching causes the creation of carbon dioxide in the blood and crystallization processes in the body.[9] Imaginative teaching brings retention of oxygen, continuous growth, because you direct their consciousness towards the future, towards life after death. Before birth, spiritual beings planted seeds of knowledge (which we now awaken through concepts), and we continue this future-oriented gesture by planting in the children's soul imaginations that will grow into the future because we are activating the will pole.

Thus we continue the work of spiritual beings when we bring living pictures, and a feeling for this reality will give our education the necessary consecration. *"Without this we cannot educate at all."*

Endnotes

2 Observations regarding the field of psychology in 1919:
At the outset of Lecture 2, Rudolf Steiner speaks rather
disparagingly about the lack of insight regarding mental picturing
and willing in the field of psychology at that time. His direct
reference to Herbart is not an arbitrary one. According to the
Stanford Encyclopedia of Philosophy (2015), "Herbart is known
mainly today as a founding figure of modern psychology and
educational theory... Indeed, without Herbart, the landscape of
modern psychology and philosophy would be unrecognizable."
Playing such a central role in the then relatively new field of study,
Herbart's very abstract, mathematical approach to understanding
the human soul and educational processes was seen by Rudolf
Steiner as a true hindrance to a more dynamic, living grasp of the
human being. (See his description of Herbart's way of thinking in
Riddles of Philosophy, CW 21.)

Steiner's more general critique of early 20th century
psychology refers, in particular—as the context in this lecture
makes clear—to the concepts of mental picturing and willing. This
should be no surprise when one considers the cosmic dimensions
of mental picturing and willing that Rudolf Steiner develops as
the lecture unfolds. Such an understanding goes far beyond what
one would expect of a modern psychologist, not only in 1919 but
today as well. These perspectives presuppose the development of
a spiritual science in Rudolf Steiner's sense of that term.

This was clear to his listeners, who were not only very familiar
with the ideas of anthroposophy, but were also highly educated
individuals regarding the contemporary thought of their time.
They would not, therefore, take Steiner's comments on modern
psychology as a superficial denunciation of modern efforts in that
field. His listeners knew well, for example, that Rudolf Steiner's

recently published book, *Riddles of the Soul* (1917), devoted 50 pages to the exploration of the ideas developed by Franz Brentano in his writings on *Psychology from an Empirical Perspective*. Steiner considered Brentano's observations regarding the nature of "intentionality" and the subtleties involved in the forming of judgments to be highly significant and seminal.

Steiner's audience knew well that Rudolf Steiner was open to and recognized the important efforts of many contemporary thinkers. But in the context of this lecture and the concepts of mental picturing and will as the basis for a new form of education, he needed to point out their limitations. From a different perspective, Steiner would have surely received with praise many of the insights that have since arisen in the field of psychology. One thinks of the developmental insights brought forth by Piaget, for example, or of the valuable perspectives of psychologists such as Abraham Maslow, Victor Frankl, Thomas Moore and James Hillman, not to mention the widely read works on multiple intelligence (Howard Gardner), on emotional intelligence (Daniel Goleman), on creative intelligence (Laurence Steinberg), to name only a few. Steiner would have certainly highlighted and supported much that is positive in these and many other efforts that have come forth as the field of psychology has unfolded in the 20th and 21st centuries. (It should also be noted that a very interesting exploration into the similarities and differences between Steiner's findings and those of depth psychology can be found in Gerhard Wehr's book, *Jung and Steiner—the Birth of a New Psychology,* 2003.)

Resources: Stanford Encyclopedia of Psychology (2015);
Steiner (1917, 2012); Wehr (2003)

3   Sensory images: the result of will-based imagination:
Rudolf Steiner's statement regarding the will-based nature
of sensory experience, as neuroscience now shows, has a
physiological basis as well. This contrasts with the everyday view
of visual perception that goes something like this: An image of
the tree is received by the retina (albeit upside down) and then
projected to the visual cortex of the brain, where the image must
somehow be reproduced and made conscious.

In reality, the retinal image is projected doubly onto the
visual cortex of the occipital lobes of both brain hemispheres and
split into four quadrants. From there the image fragments are
distributed to different parts of the cortex depending on whether
they involve shape or color or space or movement. The image of
the tree that was our starting point has been totally taken apart
by our visual system. "If we attempted to piece it back together
on the surface of the brain, the result would be a completely
distorted, unrecognizable, virtually shapeless thing bearing no
resemblance to the image we experienced." (Rohen, 2007, p. 7)
Nowhere in the brain is the image to be found as a whole. Our
sensory system focuses on dissection and analysis. This holds not
only for vision, but for our other senses, as well.

A resynthesis capable of "putting Humpty Dumpty back
together again" requires the imagination-based organizing
activity of the mind. Without this—to use Steiner's example—the
total separation of the chalk's shape from its white color could
never be overcome.

Philosophers have long known, of course, that
the way we see the world—or just an abstract part
of it like the Perspex cube (right)—depends on how
we take hold of our perceptions with the organizing/imaginative
activity of our mind. Depending on how we do this, we can see
the Perspex cube from above or from below, or as a polygon-like

gem, or as a mere series of lines. The activity of the mind engaged in composing these lines this way or that is will-activity. What changes is not the sensory data as such, but how that data is composed. (See Barfield [1988] regarding the significance of such "figuration.")

Central here is the distinction between (a) the product of our thinking activity, which are thoughts or composed images, from which we can distance ourselves in antipathy and experience as a finished product, and (b) the thinking/imaginative/organizing activity itself. Of the latter we are not conscious. We are one with it in sympathy; we cannot distance ourselves from it; it remains "the unobserved element of our normal spiritual lives." (*Philosophy of Freedom*, chapter 3) What we wake up to is the result of that activity, and that waking up requires forces of antipathy.

Resources: Holdrege (2009); Rohen (2007); Barfield (1988); Hanson (1958)

4 Human blood constantly dying: Rudolf Steiner describes here how it is the will's nature to remain seed-like, which means it must be perishing already as it is coming into being. He then describes how the bodily basis of this seed-like will in the human body, the blood, must show this same characteristic—and indeed it does. The erythrocytes or red blood cells (RBCs), which make up over 99% of all cellular elements in human blood are already dying as they are still developing. During the final normoblast and reticulocyte phases of their development, the RBCs lose their nucleus and most other organelles (ribosomes, mitochondria, etc.). Without nucleus or ribosomes the cells cannot reproduce themselves or make proteins. Without mitochondria they can only process glucose without oxygen (an interesting irony, since RBCs are the primary carriers of oxygen in the body!). As a result of this,

RBCs have a life span of only 120 days. When we consider that the blood of a normal sized human adult contains around 25 trillion RBCs, we come to the amazing fact, alluded to by Rudolf Steiner, that the RBCs are constantly dying—at a rate of about 2.5 million per second! (During the time it took you to read this paragraph you lost some 150 million of your RBCs!) At the same time, your body will have produced 150 million RBCs to replace those that passed away. This represents an unbelievable dynamic of dying and coming-into-being that takes place constantly within us, lifelong!

Another defining characteristic of the red blood cells is their non-self-centered, peripheral orientation. They are disk-shaped, with the center pinched in from both sides (biconcave), which gives them a surface area to volume ratio (SA/V) of 1.5 million to 1. Taken together, the total surface area of all the body's RBCs (there are 260 million in a single drop!) is 2000 times that of our skin! This enormous SA/V ratio shows how strongly RBCs are oriented toward the selfless task of receiving oxygen on their surface (at the sacrifice of their nucleus, which makes this possible) and how open they are to the life processes of the organs through which they constantly circulate.

Resources: Tortora & Derrickson (2013); Marieb & Hoehn (2012); Van De Graaff & Fox (1998)

5   Nerves: dying and depositing matter
a) Constantly Dying

Neurons are organized in such a way that they repeatedly go through a kind of death process followed by a renewal. At the death of the human body, chemical and physical laws of the outer world take over and the soul-spiritual is freed. A microcosm of this takes place in the transmission of a nerve impulse.

When a neuron is not stimulated (has no impulse to transmit) its membrane remains polarized, with a positive electrical charge on the outside and a negative charge on the inside. It has "resting potential." In this condition, the membrane contains predominantly sodium ions on its outer surface and potassium ions within. When a stimulus reaches the resting neuron, channels in the membrane open and sodium ions flow into the cell while potassium ions flow out. The neuron is depolarized and a voltage pulse is transmitted along the cell membrane. The inflow of sodium ions is "essentially a catabolic, dying-off process... a tiny death." (Rohen 2007) The results are not catastrophic because the neuron is able to summon up the energy to recharge its membrane by "pumping" the sodium ions back out of the cell and moving potassium ions back in. This regenerative process is metabolic in nature. (At the actual death of the body as a whole, these regenerative, energy-transport processes cease. Sodium ions then flow into the cell, differences in concentration are eliminated, and the cells fill with fluid and die.)

From the perspective taken by Rudolf Steiner in this lecture, this brief catabolic death process frees soul forces, a micro-version of what happens at death itself, when the soul is freed from the body and goes its own way. These recurring death events at the neuron level are the prerequisite for the awakening of consciousness.

b) Depositing Matter

Whereas the pulsing, surging flow of blood through our body represents a continuous renewal of life-giving forces, the nerves present a very different picture. What we find along the pathways of much of our nervous system is a deposition of very dense and inactive, white lipoprotein known as myelin that forms sheaths around the nerve fibers (axons). These layers consist to 80% of metabolically extremely inactive, strongly mineralized, crystal-like lipid deposits. Myelin insulates the nerve fibers and allows nerve impulses to travel more rapidly. These myelin sheaths give the name to what is known as the "white matter" of the brain and spinal cord. The myelination of nerve fibers in the central and peripheral nervous systems stands in contrast to the unmyelinated vegetative nerves (gray matter) that operate outside the sphere of our conscious influence.

Resources: Wolff (2014); Tortora & Derrickson (2013); Constanzo (2013); Marieb & Hoehn (2012); Rohen (2007)

6   Efferent (motoric) nerves: In countering the orthodox view that movements are caused by the so-called motor neurons (efferent neurons), Rudolf Steiner is not questioning the empirical data regarding the two nerve types (afferent and efferent) identified by conventional science, but rather the interpretation of their functions within the human organization. Whereas the standard view for centuries has been that the brain is the organ of consciousness and thus the foundation of all "inner life" (soul life), Rudolf Steiner in *Study of Man* and elsewhere reports on a threefold manner in which the human soul dwells within the body. He describes in these lectures that our reflective, waking consciousness has its seat primarily in the central nervous system, our feeling life in the rhythmic processes of breathing and circulation, and our will in the metabolic-limb activity.

This revolutionary perspective has been investigated and further delineated by several generations of anthroposophical physicians and biologists (Hensel, Rohen, Wolff, Kranich, Schad, among others), leading to a rich literature on this theme, albeit mostly in the German language. One helpful elucidation of the topic that has been translated into English can be found in the book *Functional Morphology* (2007) by Professor Dr. Med. Johannes Rohen, author of several well-known medical textbooks in the German language. What follows is a short description of a few main points found in Rohen's book.

Although nerves are always found bundled together with both efferent and afferent nerves present, Rohen shows in considerable detail how the threefold nature of the nervous system is clearly evident in the human being. In the head region (brain), the sensory system is dominant with afferent nerves in the foreground and the efferent (motor) nerves playing a secondary regulative role. The opposite is found in the autonomic nervous system, where efferent neurons are primary and afferent less prominent. In the spinal column a relatively harmonious balance is found between the two neuron types.

At the will-pole of our organization, Rohen explains, the activity of the inner organs is not actually caused by the nervous system. Blood circulation, hormone secretion, intestinal activity, and much more takes place without the nervous system. The primary task of the autonomic neurons in this realm is to ensure that the organs are sensitive to the activity of each other and thus able to coordinate and harmonize their activities.

Similarly, the efferent spinal nerves of the middle system—which are in contact with the striated skeletal muscles—are not the primary cause of muscle contraction, for this is largely dependent on metabolic processes within the muscle cells. The nervous system's function here is—once again—to bring the activity of the many muscles involved in any coordinated movement into harmony with each other. When, for example, any muscle group contracts, another group of muscles must extend in coordination with it or cramping and movement disturbances arise. The cause of the movement is will activity (based on metabolic processes), but the coordination thereof depends on efferent (motor) neurons.

Between these two poles of metabolic will activity and the central nervous system lies the rhythmical system (breathing and circulation). Every muscle must be well provided with a blood flow that brings energy-laden nutrients—primarily glucose—and oxygen. This rhythmical component of the movement system can be seen in relation to our feeling life, for every truly human (non-mechanical) movement involves a feeling-element, as well.

Resources: Schad (2014); Wolff (2014); Rohen (2007, 2001)

7   **Synapses:** The gaps Rudolf Steiner is referring to are commonly known as synapses, gaps where nerve activity is interrupted and the impulse must "spring" from one neuron to the next. The gap (synaptic cleft) is a fluid-filled space that separates the axon of one neuron from the dendrite of the next. (Axons lead the nerve impulse away from the cell body of the neuron; dendrites carry the impulse received from an axon to the cell body of the next neuron.)

   To traverse the synaptic gap, a chemical known as a neurotransmitter must be released into the synapse, which then moves across the gap to the membrane of the post-synaptic neuron (dendrite) that is to receive the nerve impulse. If it is an "excitatory" neurotransmitter, the impulse will be taken up by the post-synaptic neuron and transmitted further. If the neurotransmitter is an "inhibitory" one, the impulse will not be carried on beyond the synapse. After such an event, a short period of time must pass before the synapse can be reengaged.

   These synapses—that connect or separate different neurons and neuron groups—enable the nervous system's great variety of functional possibilities. (Single neurons can have anywhere from 1000 to 10,000 synaptic connections with other neurons!) The number of synaptic connections determines ultimately the nervous system's level of differentiation. More highly developed nervous systems are more adaptable because the number of potential connections they can establish (and/or dissolve) is greater. Mastering new skills requires establishing new neural connections and abandoning old ones. Repeated or continuous use of a synapse enhances the pre-synaptic neuron's ability to excite the post-synaptic neuron, thereby increasing the efficiency of neurotransmission. In this way, the human brain remains flexible (neural plasticity) into old age. In animals these connections become essentially fixed after an initial imprinting phase.

Flexibility and dynamic pulsing are characteristics of the rhythmical system. The alternating dissolution and reestablishing of synaptic activity is a manifestation of the rhythmical system in the nervous system. At the soul level, dissolving and connecting are an expression of antipathy and sympathy. Careful observation also confirms that all conceptual capacity is accompanied by a stronger or weaker resonance in the feeling life. Judgments receive their conviction based on the feeling component that informs them.

Resources: Tortora & Derrickson (2013); Marieb & Hoehn (2012); Rohen (2001)

8 Gray matter: Rudolf Steiner describes here how the outer layer of the brain—which consists of gray matter—functions as the metabolic pole of the brain, by nourishing and regenerating the neurons after the catabolic ("death") processes that make consciousness possible.

Gray matter is composed mostly of neuron cell bodies or soma, non-neuron brain cells known as glial cells, and capillaries. Compared to other cells, the soma of a neuron is very large. It resembles a gland cell, but one that produces great amounts of protein. This protein is not secreted, however, but maintains a constant centrifugal flow outward to the neuron's peripheral formations, such as synapses. Catabolic products are then returned to the soma via retrograde, centripetal flow, where they are re-synthesized. The centrifugal and centripetal plasma flow in the nerve fibers run parallel to each other and enable the re-enlivening processes that make ongoing nerve activity possible.

The glial cells are also central to the gray matter in that they transport nutrients and energy to the neurons. They also provide a stabilized chemical environment around the neurons by "mopping up" excess chemicals, recycling released neurotransmitters, and detoxifying the chemical milieu. Glial cells are also known as "nanny cells" due to these supportive functions.

Resources: Marieb & Hoehn (2012); Rohen (2007, 2001)

9   **CO$_2$ retention:** Rudolf Steiner indicates that a one-sided focus on conceptual activity leads to CO$_2$ retention. As we have seen (see endnote 1), with intensified thought activity respiratory movement slows down (hypoventilation). As a consequence, the venous blood-flow slows or stops, causing CO$_2$ retention at above normal levels. This leads to an accumulation of breakdown products—CO$_2$ being just one of them—that are carried by the venous blood, with an accompanying decrease in blood pH levels and tissue metabolism that tends toward the acidic. (If it becomes more extreme, this malady is known as respiratory acidosis.)

Resources: Husemann (2013); Constanzo (2013)

Commentary: Thinking cognition and will

In this lecture, Rudolf Steiner works with thinking cognition and will. Thinking is based on inner mental picturing of what we experienced in the past life. (We can also look at the past in our current life.) This is experienced through imagery. For example, if we reflect on our childhood, an image of ourselves playing in the sand arises. This process of reflection is antipathy in which we step back in our mind and reflect. Through this process memory arises.

When we unite ourselves with something, we use sympathy forces. An imagination arises, a mental picture of something outside ourselves. This becomes a seed for the future and is experienced as will. For example, the teacher may be telling the children about a hero who took care of injured animals. Through vivid descriptions, the child unites in sympathy and wants to be like that person. The child's will is activated to do something similar, whether it is in a future life or in the present one.

Steiner advises the teachers not to ask too many intellectual questions about the past as these relate to experiences that are dead; they tire the memory. Instead the teacher should give the child as many imaginative stories as possible, as these awaken the feelings and stimulate the will.

Toward the end of the lecture Rudolf Steiner focuses on the threefold aspect of the body: head, chest and digestive-limb systems. These cannot be experienced separately as they are interconnected. For example, although most of the sense organs are found in the head (eyes, ears, nose, mouth), the sense of touch and warmth are felt all over the body.

Study Questions

1. How is "soul breathing" connected to sympathy and antipathy?
2. Describe the polarity of the human being regarding nerve and blood poles.
3. What does Steiner mean by true Imagination?
4. Why must we love something in order to know it? How does this process work?
5. What activities in our teaching help the child form memory and concepts? strengthen the will?

6. How can we, as teachers in the classroom, use a balance of sympathy and antipathy?

7. How is a child's tendency toward antipathy (nerve-pole too strong) and sympathy (blood pole too strong) revealed through various activities? (e.g., movement, play, form drawing, drawing, painting, sculpting, writing, singing, music, eurythmy, handwork, classroom engagement, etc.)

8. How should a teacher balance enthusiastic engagement with reflective observation in different activities and at different grade levels?

9. How does your enthusiasm for a subject help the children learn?

10. Give examples of teaching with images in any of the following: storytelling; movement or circle time; a painting lesson; form drawing; geometry; geography; science; history.

Lecture 3
August 23, 1919

Modern teachers must have a comprehensive view of cosmic law and of the highest ideals of humanity. Teachers of all grade levels and subjects should be viewed as equally important and worthy, especially regarding their spiritual character. As human beings we exist both as natural and as spiritual beings, and we bring both nature and spirit to the child.

Psychology suffers from the Catholic dogma of the dual nature of the human being, ignoring the true threefold reality.[10] This view assumed an egregiously harmful form through the Law of the Conservation of Energy (which is actually a misunderstanding of J.R. Mayer's research focus), which asserts that no new energy can ever be created. But, in fact, in the human being new energy and even new matter can be (and are) created.[11]

As teachers we need to guide pupils toward an understanding of both nature and spiritual life. Nature appears to us from two sides: as ideas (laws) and as sense perceptions. The latter have the character of will. For this reason, nature appears to have two parts, and therefore the belief that the human body is also twofold. Laws of nature, discovered through reason, point toward what is in the process of dying. When the senses are directed towards nature, that process has a will nature. (The etheric "arms" of the eyes "touch" what we see.) Our spiritual sense of Self arises because our eyes can meet, as in the eurythmic "O."

The senses' will nature is especially evident in the senses of touch, taste and smell. There we see a connection with the metabolism in a higher sense.

Dead laws of nature become a part of us, but what we comprehend as nature's becoming, its future, enters into us through the will-nature of the senses. Nature continuously dies and becomes. We comprehend the dying through the intellect, which is connected to life before birth. We comprehend the becoming through the senses, which are connected to life after death.

If human beings were unable to save something from pre-earthly life in the form of thoughts, then freedom would not be possible. They would either connect with dying nature or with its mere seed aspect. But beyond the comprehension of the dead through the intellect and the becoming through the will, there is something that only human beings possess: pure thinking, thinking that grasps the supersensible. In sense-free thinking, in which the will is always present, the human being gains a proper understanding of his relationship to the dying and becoming of nature.

Modern science can see only those two aspects, dying and becoming, and a point of clarity about the differing perspectives of natural and spiritual science is reached by asking: What is the significance of human existence for nature? For natural science, there is simply no significance; if human beings did not exist, nature would be just the same as it is. But for spiritual science, animals, especially the higher ones, were separated from the evolving human species in the course of evolution, and if humanity did not exist, then animals, and the earth itself, would look quite different.[12] The minerals would have crumbled long ago if it were not for human corpses releasing forces at death that allow the continuation of the crystallization processes, and plants would have lost their ability to grow. In reality, human corpses act like yeast for the earth. By incorporating a spirit into an earthly body, a human being endows earth existence with a yeast-like impetus for the continuation of formative and life processes.

41

Thus earth is a whole system, with the human being an intrinsic and essential aspect of it. Even at death, the human being stands within the cosmic process. The material aspect of her body has been permeated with spirit, and at death the transformed matter endows the earth with new forces, coming from the supersensible world. Without human beings, the earth would long since have died.

The death processes operating in nature, which are countered to some degree by human corpses, are acting on the human body as well. Left to influence the body strongly, they become the bones, the skeletal system; when they are arrested to some degree, they become the nerves. The nerves "want" to become bone, but are stopped short by other processes (see below) in the body. This is one polarity: Death processes become nerves and bone.

The opposite, life-giving process manifests in muscles and blood. Those prevent the nerves from calcifying into bone. In rickets, for example, they act too powerfully, thus preventing sufficient hardening to take place in the bones. So health depends on a proper balance between bone and nerve, on the one hand, and blood and muscles on the other. In the eye we see an example of how the bone process retreats, leaving behind only its weaker "cousin," the nerves, and how those connect with the muscles and blood in the eye to facilitate its proper functioning.

The ancients understood that people think with their bones as well as nerves. Geometry and other abstract sciences arise out of subtle movements of the finer bodies, which are perceived subconsciously by the skeleton. A triangle, for example, is a series of supersensible movements perceived by the skeleton due to our upright position. Other geometric movements are performed by the earth itself, and all geometric forms, including the solid ones, are supersensible occurrences made visible.

So we have the dying, grasped through the intellect, and the becoming, grasped unconsciously through the will. The becoming processes depend on the human being, and without the human being they would cease and the earth would die.

The human soul is not a mere observer of nature and the world, but a stage on which cosmic events play out. The interplay of the nerve-bone pole with the muscle-blood pole continuously creates new energy and new matter, saving the earth from dying. The blood, through its connection with the nerves, creates new matter and energy. Though nothing arises out of nothing, things can cease to exist, and new things can arise in the process of transformation within the human being.

New formulations are needed for the realities of life. Instead of abstract laws and definitions, we need to characterize what the reality in front of us reveals. For example, rather than the Impermeability Law, a description: Those bodies or beings are impermeable, whose nature it is that where they are in space no other being of the same nature can be at the same time. This is a description of what our observation actually gives us, rather than an abstract law.

Endnotes

10 The Eighth Ecumenical Council of Constantinople: Rudolf Steiner points to the Eighth Ecumenical Council (869 AD) as a symptomatic historic event because it called for the replacement of a deeper threefold (trichotomy) view of the human being as consisting of body, soul and spirit with a twofold (dichotomy) view in which the human being possesses only body and soul. This dogmatic proclamation contained in the 11th Canon of the Eighth Ecumenical Council has had the long-term historical consequence—says Rudolf Steiner—of hindering later thinkers from developing true insight into the nature of the human being. Although it is only briefly mentioned in this lecture, Steiner considered this Council to have such historical reverberations that he referred to it in some 40 lectures between the years 1904 and 1924.

What view did the Council's decision replace? Although there were many perspectives and nuances to be found in earlier thinkers, most influential were the Greek philosophers Plato and Aristotle, who both distinguished between body (*soma*), soul (*psyche*) and spirit (*pneuma*). This threefold picture also lived on (in many different shades) in the Christian tradition up until the 9th century (Dietz, 1990).

If, however, the spirit is no longer seen as a characteristic of the individual human being—as the Council proclaimed—then spiritual guidance for the individual must come from without. In contrast to such a view, Rudolf Steiner in his book *Theosophy* characterizes the spirit as that part of the human being which transcends the subjective soul life and can (potentially) grasp the things of the world in their true being. The spirit (in contrast to the soul) strives to grasp what *is* and not what merely *pleases or displeases*. In the soul alone we are unable to transcend our own subjectivity; we are limited to our own personal, self-referencing perspective on the world. Through our spirit the lawfulness of things and beings can speak to us, and therein lies the potential for becoming a "free human being."

A concept of the human being devoid of spirit sees the soul as primarily oriented toward the bodily, where drives and passions hold sway. Such a perspective can lead easily to views of the human being such as those found in Darwinism, psychoanalysis, and so forth.

If the human is no longer seen as capable of penetrating into the deeper reality of things through spiritual striving, then the world becomes something foreign. We become spectators of, rather than participants in, the world as thinking beings. The only viable approach to knowledge then becomes the experimental method. Knowledge must come primarily from experimental data that can be first understood with the help of statistical analysis. As the famous behavioral psychologist, B.F. Skinner, put it: The human soul is only a "black box." We cannot understand it, we can only modify the behaviors that come from it with the help of rewards and punishments that we apply to it.

Resources: Leber (2002); Dietz (1990); Lindenberg (1981)

11 The conservation of energy: After addressing the hindrances that a dualistic understanding of the human being provides for a true psychology, Rudolf Steiner now turns to the consequences of a one-sided monistic view of the forces of nature. Although Mayer himself was interested in the metamorphosis of forces and not an abstract law regarding the conservation of energy, it is the latter that lives on in our time. The law is not problematic in its narrower sense as an insight into the transformation of one energy form into another, but rather in the tendency it has to "close our eyes" to phenomena of transformation and metamorphosis in the sense world. This "conservation of energy" mindset easily leads one to the conclusion that nothing new can ever come into being. The emphasis on energy transformation keeps us from seeing that, as Rudolf Steiner (1920) puts it, "When somewhere a form arises, it is, in fact, a new creation. We can see this literally when from out of a liquid a solid form comes into being. The form appears visibly as a new creation, and it disappears again when it melts back in the fluidity."

How difficult a straightforward phenomenological approach to nature is for the modern mind becomes apparent when we consider how Frits Julius (2000) describes what the phenomena actually show us when we observe a chemical experiment.

> We start with a yellow powder (sulfur) and a shiny metallic powder (iron), which are mixed in a certain proportion. Then we heat a part of this mass so it starts to glow; the glow spreads and "eats" through the whole mass. As long as we had a mixture, we could separate both powders quite easily. Both still had their characteristic properties: Iron was magnetic, sulfur could easily be melted or even vaporized (sublimated). After they have combined, we obtain an inseparable mass, with totally new properties. All properties of iron and sulfur have disappeared, except that of mass. If some dilute hydrochloric acid is poured over the iron sulfide, then hydrogen sulfide gas is evolved that is recognizable by its awful smell—that is a new property; the fusibility and the magnetic properties have disappeared.
>
> This fact is really appreciated when we realize that in such a process the principle of impenetrability of matter is negated. Initially both substances were next to each other and not in each other. When they combined, they both entered the same space... (Julius, 55–56) It is a most remarkable phenomenon that during a chemical reaction the "impenetrability" of matter is overcome, and two different substances become a complete new unity... The properties by which we recognize the substances taking part in the reaction disappear, and totally new substances with new properties emerge. Only one property, the weight (mass), has remained the same... Substances are recognized by their properties, but these disappear during a chemical reaction; which means that the "chemicals" themselves vanish and new ones appear in their place. (Julius, 70–71)

In the words of Rudolf Steiner:

> By describing light, heat, etc., as "energy," we have
> disregarded all the details which are specific for the
> various senses and only taken into account a general
> property, common to them all. (1950, 261)

To which Julius concludes:

> In a way, in terms of "energy," it makes no difference
> if it occurs as electricity, heat, or light. Energy is,
> therefore, a common unit for forces, in the same
> way that money is for the exchange of goods. Here
> also—as often is the case—we see the tendency to
> think the opposite to truth. We imagine that energy is
> the real thing, and the acting forces of nature only its
> manifestations. (Julius, 70)

Resources: Leber (2002); Julius (2000); Steiner (1950, 1920)

12 Evolution: With his statement that, at a particular stage in
the earth's evolution, humans were once one with the animal world
and that then the animal world was "precipitated out," Steiner
touches on an enormous topic that he has already developed in
detail in *Esoteric Science*. Such a statement appears to "turn the
whole world on its head" in relation to the Darwinist picture
of evolution that is presupposed by most educated individuals
of the 20th and 21st centuries (with a few exceptions like the
resurgence of Creationism in conservative Christian circles).

Less widely known, however, are significant developments
in evolutionary biology since the high point of the neo-Darwinist
Modern Synthesis in the mid- and late 20th century. Many
biologists have since moved beyond Darwin's one-sided emphasis
on the influence of external forces (natural selection through
random variation) in evolution.

47

An important catalyst to these new perspectives was the book *Ontogeny and Phylogeny* by Harvard biologist Stephen Jay Gould. A highly influential thinker in the field of evolutionary theory, Gould reawakened interest in the connection between the biological development of individual organisms (ontogeny) and the evolutionary history of an organism (phylogeny). During the last third of the 20th century many new perspectives on the nature of evolutionary development arose, in particular a new branch of evolutionary theory known as Evo-Devo (evolutionary developmental biology). Evo-Devo focuses on variations in the timing and rate of development (heterochrony) as the generator of countless new developmental possibilities.

This approach to evolution was awarded its first Nobel Prize in 1995, and research in this direction has exploded since then. It would go far beyond the scope of this text to explain in detail the findings of this perspective, but suffice it to say that the idea of random natural selection has given way to the discovery of deep commonalities (homologies) that connect very different species and the idea that certain internally determined growth and differentiation processes are shared across a wide range of species.

In the words of Cliff Tabin, a developmental and evolutionary biologist at Harvard Medical School:

> One of the most amazing surprises over the time I've been in science has been the finding that the genes that are involved in making animals as different as a fruit fly and a human being are fundamentally the same genes. When we thought about such things, say, 20 years ago, one had to assume that the genes to make a fruit fly would include instructions for wings, genes that we didn't need. And, conversely, that we'd have genes dedicated to making a human limb or human heart that

a fly would never have. The stunning finding was that, to a first approximation, the same genes are present in both and are being used in both.

For that worm to evolve into a fly, or to evolve ultimately into a human, those genes were used in different ways, in different combinations, with different timing.

Fundamentally, the genetic toolkit, as we call it, was already there in the common ancestor. And that ancestral set of genes was powerful and versatile enough to provide the material for generating the diverse forms of animal life we now see on Earth. That was something that nobody expected, and it's made the study of various organisms very profound. It means what you learn from studying the development of a fly really has direct implications for understanding the way we are made ourselves, because as different as a fly is from a human and as long ago as we diverged, we're using basically the same genes to do the same thing—to make organization emerge in an embryo. (Nova 2009)

This is a very different picture of evolution than the one most people still carry around with them. It grows much closer to the idea of an archetype in the sense of Goethe—of a living principle that can bring forth the most varied forms. It is easy to fixate on the "gene level" of things, and that was the case for most of 20th-century biology, but in the meantime the question is much more: How is it that essentially the same raw material—the physical substrate of heredity known as the "genetic toolkit"— can be "expressed" in such amazing variety? As Ernst-Michael Kranich once put it: Genes are like the keyboard to the pianist. The questions then become: Who is playing the piano (causing the keys to bring forth this or that kind of music), and who wrote the music in the first place?

Modern biologists are far from concluding that the composer and pianist of evolution can be found in the evolution of the human being—that the human archetype is the whole, from which the great diversity of the animal world as one-sided expressions of that archetype evolved. But the modern, Evo-Devo perspective—that focuses on developmental dynamics and not on random natural selection—certainly brings this within the realm of possibility.

Parallel to and in harmony with these developments in mainstream evolutionary biology, scientists working from a Goetheanistic/anthroposophical perspective have produced a rich literature on these questions. To name several key resources available in English:

Holdrege, C. (2005). *The Giraffe's Long Neck*. Nature Institute Perspectives #4.

Kipp, F. (2005). *Childhood and Human Evolution*. Hillsdale, NY: Adonis.

Kranich, E. (1999) *Thinking Beyond Darwin*. Hudson, NY: Lindisfarne.

Poppelbaum, H. (2014). *Man and Animal*. UK: Rudolf Steiner Press.

Rosslenbroich, B. (2014). *The Origin of Autonomy*. New York: Springer.

Schad, W. (1977). *Man and Mammals*. Garden City, NY: Waldorf Press.

Suchantke, A. (2009). *Metamorphosis: Evolution in Action*. Hillsdale, NY: Adonis.

Verhulst, J. (2003). *Developmental Dynamics in Humans and Other Primates*. Hillsdale, NY: Adonis.

The Nature Institute. http://natureinstitute.org

The details to this rich topic, and how they might support Steiner's "revolutionary" statement that animals presuppose human development, cannot be developed here. In conclusion, may the words of evolutionary biologist and anthroposophist, Professor Dr. Wolfgang Schad, point to how open the question of evolutionary origins has become today:

> Have animals descended from plants, vertebrate animals from invertebrates, mammals from reptiles, humans from apes? We are accustomed to hearing the question of evolution (descendance) put in such a simple manner. And yet nothing today is more certain than that none of today's living invertebrate animals are ancestors of the vertebrates. Nor is it the case that today's mammals are descendants of the lower vertebrates, or that humans have descended from today's apes. As obvious as this is after taking a close look at the evidence, it is all the more important to recognize the fundamental relationship it reveals: Humans, apes and the other mammals, etc., have all developed out of a common—today not existent—ancestor. That alone is the basis for the obvious relationships that these forms reveal to each other.

Resources: Schad (2012); Nova (2009); Amundson (2007); Carroll (2005); Gould (2002, 1977); Bauer & Holdrege (1985); Davy (1985)

Commentary: Nature

Rudolf Steiner focuses on our relationship to nature. He raises a high bar for teachers, especially in the lower grades, to have a connection with the highest ideas of humanity. He expects teachers to have an extensive background in the laws of the universe. Is this referring to the influence of spiritual beings?

Teachers of all grade levels, including kindergarten, should be regarded as equal in every way. With this statement, Steiner sets a tone for colleagueship within the faculty as well as for financial considerations. This is a challenge today as some Waldorf schools are following the mainstream practice of offering higher wages to high school teachers and to those with advanced degrees.

As teachers we bring to the children the world of nature on one hand and the world of spirit on the other. By living with the seasons, walking in the forest, gathering seeds and observing birds, the children feel a connection to space and time. Through appropriate stories, children can connect the ideals of the characters with something of a higher order. The sciences point the way to the world of nature and the humanities to the world of spirit. This understanding is necessary for the children to take a place in the social life in which they live.

It is important to clear up the comment about the Law of the Conservation of Energy or Force because it is mentioned in many of the education lectures. This First Law of Thermodynamics states that the sum of all energies or forces present in the universe is constant, that these forces only undergo certain changes. Steiner makes the point that, while this is true for the mineral, plant and animal world, it is not true for the human world because human beings are always creating new possibilities that have not been there before. This relates to the major points he makes in *Philosophy of Freedom*.

One of the most significant statements for the teacher to work with is that what we understand of nature through our thinking is dead, and what we understand of nature through our senses is of the will. This statement stands behind the science lessons from first grade through twelfth. What the child observes, smells, hears and tastes before coming to concepts is a living process that is different from the usual approach which sets up a hypothesis, followed by an experiment to prove it. The principle of phenomenology is the central pedagogical approach indicated here.

Study Questions

1. In terms of sympathy and antipathy, what is the problem with modern education?

2. What can you do to "imbue yourself with the power of Imagination"?

3. Compare the two processes of meeting Nature with our thought-life and with our living will.

4. What does it mean to be active in our senses?

5. How does the human being create new life forces for the Earth?

6. What is the nature of our relationship as human beings to animals?

7. Is the "value" of teaching greater or lesser at different levels—early childhood, grade school, high school?

8. How does the idea that new forces are continually coming into existence through human beings inform our teaching?

9. How can we use the curriculum to overcome the view of the human being as, at best, a "spectator," and at worst a "despoiler" of Nature?

10. What meditations help us come to know the forces of becoming and the forces of dying away, both in Nature and in ourselves?

Lecture 4
August 25, 1919

Teachers must place a special value on the forming of the child's will and feeling. However, those are rarely understood. Feeling is held-back will, and will is feeling made active. We only understand feeling if we understand the will. As I have said, in the will there is always something that remains unresolved in us through to death.

We also look at the human being as having a physical body, the carrier of inherited traits; then there is the soul, which is the part of our pre-natal existence closest to the body, and the spiritual aspect that only manifests in modern human beings as a tendency.

The will manifests itself differently in the various members of the human constitution.

In the Spirit:

Spirit Self is a plurality after death (*manes*, the Roman spirits of the dead, is a plural noun) when it becomes interwoven with other spiritual beings.

Life Spirit and Spirit Human exist only as tendencies in present-day humanity during life on earth.

After death, these three spirit members develop towards the next incarnation, connected by a spiritual "umbilical cord" to the spiritual beings around them.

Below the spirit members are the three soul members and the three bodies. We can look at the way in which the will manifests itself in each of these:

The will appears in the **physical body** as *instinct*, as the aspect that determines conduct through the form of the body. Animals show this most clearly, as, for example, the beaver's ability to construct a dam or the bee's ability to build its honeycomb. These capacities live in the body of the animal; no schooling is necessary for their acquisition.

In the **etheric body** will appears as *drives*, which are more inward than instincts.

In the **astral body** will becomes conscious and appears as *desires*. Those are less habitual than drives and can be momentary, fleeting.

The "I" penetrates the three soul members and lives in them such that the will becomes *motive*: the signature of individualization in the will.

The spirit members take up the residue of action; here we see its seed nature.

The **Spirit Self** takes the action into a *wish* form: the wish to do better next time.

In the **Life Spirit** the wish becomes more concrete: the *intent* to do better in the future.

(An example is given from psychology books about the working of the subconscious—the "second person" within us.)

In the **Spirit Human** the *decision* arises out of the intent.

During life between birth and death, wish, intent and decision (to do better) are only thoughts; they become realities only after death.

The idea that children have the same relationships with one another as adults do is detrimental to their education and even to civilization. Children have to develop quite different powers of soul and body, particularly with regard to the will.

Teachers must understand how education affects the will: Will grown old becomes thought; will not yet developed is feeling.

Unconscious repetition strengthens the feeling. Conscious repetition strengthens the will because it increases the decision-making power. Thus it is good for children to have chores.

Artistic activity is good for the will because it requires repetition and gives fresh joy each time.

Commentary: Education of the will and feelings

The focus in this lecture is the education of the will and the feelings. Steiner describes the different states of will, e.g., instinct, impulse, desire, motive, wish, intention and resolve. The last three are experienced through mental pictures.

In other words, when the child can create an imagination of organizing his/her classroom desk, then it becomes possible to carry out this intention rather than being commanded to do it by outer authority. Or a child can form an imagination of apologizing to someone. Once the imagination is there, the child can step into it and carry out the intentions.

Teachers can differentiate the different kinds of will in the ways they ask students to carry out activities. For example, if a child is hungry, the teacher can work on his/her instincts by having the child wait for food to be passed out. If a child feels threatened, she might run away or attack another child. Learning to confront another student by using words rather than action allows the possibility to transform impulses. Working with children to verbalize their desires or motives helps them gain a sense of inward power and the skill to work out how they want to handle various situations. Clarifying intentions is a valuable approach for middle and high school students.

Another way to work on the will is for the teacher to introduce actions that have to be constantly repeated. For example, pushing in the chair quietly, raising hands, sharpening pencils at the beginning of class, watering the plants in the classroom, placing a napkin on the table before snack is handed out. Developing habits with conscious repetition cultivates the will. Speaking the birthday verse once a week cultivates feelings for the verse. The teacher has created the structure. When the child begins to do tasks because they are needed and not directed, the will is strengthened.

Whether it is reciting poetry, painting, doing form drawing, writing beautifully, playing recorder, or singing, the child fills his/her will with a sense of artistry and a feeling of joy in learning.

Study Questions

1. Why is it important that education in the future give emphasis to developing the children's will and feeling?
2. How do the seven levels of the will relate to the sevenfold human being? Which of these do we share with animals?
3. Give an example for each of the seven levels of the will.
4. As teachers, how do we reach and strengthen the will in children?
5. How can we consciously repeat activities with the students and also bring "fresh joy" to them every time?
6. Look at curriculum material and student work from a 7th grade creative writing block ("Wish, Wonder and Surprise"). In the realm of "wishing," what levels of the will can you identify?
7. Steiner comments that the "advanced" man is never self-satisfied, but always has the "soft undertone" of a wish to do better. How can that be a useful motto for teachers? How can it apply to helping children?
8. At what point does the human Will rise to a truly moral level?
9. How does a teacher "earn" authority with the children?

Lecture 5
August 26, 1919

From understanding the will we can proceed to the rest of human nature. Thinking we saw as connected with the nerves, will as connected with the activity of the blood. We can now approach feeling, but we must remember that in life the three soul forces are always mixed. (We isolate them only for clarity's sake.)

Will must be penetrated with thinking if it is not to be a dull, instinctive act, and thinking is always penetrated by will when we form thoughts, connect one thought with another, and proceed to judgment and decision. Thus will is mainly will and thinking is mainly thinking, but each has an undercurrent of the other.

The eye is an example of how both nerves and blood vessels play a role right into the periphery of the sense organization, and the same is true in the limbs.

Cognitive activity has an antipathetic nature: If the eyes did not have blood vessels, everything we saw would repel us inwardly. The blood balances the antipathy generated by the nerves.

There is more blood in animal eyes than in the human eye, and this is true of their senses in general. Thus animals live in greater sympathy with their surroundings and are, in turn, more influenced by environmental elements such as climate and season. Our antipathetically structured senses allow us the separation that makes personality possible.

Just as they flow together in cognitive activity, will and thinking work together in willing, too. Our ability to act rationally is based on the antipathy that joins our sympathy with what is wanted. Just as the full antipathy in cognition is present in exceptional cases (disgust), so sympathy is fully present in exceptional cases (devotion, enthusiasm) of willing. Usually, they balance each other so that ordinary objective action can take place.

The world is wisely created so that our antipathy remains mostly unconscious.

Children come into the world imbued with an instinctive sympathy. As educators we must permeate this sympathy with an appropriate antipathy. This antipathy can balance animalistic sympathy by introducing moral ideals. Moral ideals always have an ascetic quality—refrain from animalistic sympathies. Thus willing should be permeated with cognition.

Feeling stands midway between the poles of thinking and willing. Those two poles interpenetrate and balance one another, so separating them is difficult. Feeling is even less separate, since it is inherently a balancing situation in us.

For objective willing to rise to activity, it needs enthusiasm and love—feeling qualities. For ordinary sense activity to grow pronouncedly antipathetic (become knowledge), it needs disgust —again a feeling quality! Feeling enters into thinking as well.

The argument between Brentano and Sigwart shows that both missed the essential point. They argued about human judgment, with Brentano's thinking that feeling plays no part in objective judgment and Sigwart's saying that judgment always contains feeling. The truth has to be seen in the interaction between the soul forces: The objective content of judgment lies outside the feeling life, but for an individual to be convinced of the correctness of the judgment, feeling (of evidence) must arise.

This is an example of how exact concepts have to be developed by first developing ourselves through anthroposophy [schooling of consciousness].

Feeling radiates its essence in the direction of both willing and thinking, but remains, in a sense, incomplete thinking and willing. It is thinking in reserve and feeling in reserve. Sympathy and antipathy, which remain hidden in the poles, become evident in feeling. Feeling becomes conscious when the interplay of blood and nerves becomes conscious near the center of the body's activity. Thus, in the eye, which is separated into its own bony socket, we don't notice the sympathy and antipathy. But in the ear, which is much more integrated into the body, separating the sense impression from the feeling it arouses becomes more difficult.[13] The argument between Wagner, who saw music as an expression mainly of feeling, and Hanslick, who saw it as a pure connection of tone to tone, pitted two one-sided views against one another. In reality, the senses permeate the periphery of the human being with cognitive activity, and feelings are always a part of that: The human being becomes a being of feeling.

Modern desires to create a theory of sensory activity are founded on the inexact knowledge of the senses. True knowledge should guide us to consider one sense at a time, since each one is unique. Only a path of knowledge grounded in what is outlined in my philosophical works (the marriage of perceptions with thinking activity) can lead to true knowledge. Reality is not given to us in its totality from the beginning. It is what we win through our activity of knowing, gradually, and is not reflected in us whole, as Kant said. We meet true reality only in the spirit world (after death or through initiation), and on earth we have to "conquer" it.

Endnotes

13 Eye and ear: As Rudolf Steiner points out here, the organs of the eye and ear are very different in structure and in how they relate to the rest of the body. This is evident from the very outset of their development. Eye development begins with the lateral walls of the forebrain (proencephalon) bulging out (diverticulation) and then growing toward the outer surface of the body (ectoderm). Once there, each bulge (optic vesicle) invaginates to create a cup-like form, the optic cup. Into this cup the surface ectoderm thickens and invaginates, forming what will become the lens of the eye. In the back of the cup, the retina and blood-vessel-containing choroid layer forms. Where eye development is strongly a movement from the inside out toward the surface—with a modest response thereto from the periphery through the formation of the lens—the ear develops from the outside in. This process has too many aspects to describe here, but the end-result is an organ with three functionally distinct sections: the outer, middle and inner ear.

Whereas the presence of blood vessels in the eye is restricted to an area at the back behind the retina, in the ear, the eardrum is already well supplied with blood vessels. Connected to the inside of the eardrum is a sequence of three tiny bones, the ossicles. Well known as hammer, anvil and stirrup, they are connected to each other by real joints, forming the smallest limb (by far!) in the human body. In contrast to our other muscle-guided and gravity-overcoming limbs, these tiny bones are moved by sound itself!

Moving to the inner ear—to which the stirrup connects—we come to a fluid-filled spiral canal of two-and-a-half turns (the cochlea), which is embedded at the base of the skull in the hardest bone of the body (the petrous bone). The inner ear is filled with and surrounded by watery lymph, as are the brain and spinal cord (as we saw in endnote 1), and is connected to that cerebrospinal space. The impulses that pass from the eardrum to the ossicles and the inner ear move through as so-called "traveling waves." High pitches produce waves that break early on in the cochlea, deeper tones carry further. At the place where a wave breaks, a sensory cell is stimulated.

The fact that the ear's sensory receptors are not already located on the eardrum, but are found only after the limb activity of the ossicles has been transferred into fluid channels in the densest part of the human body (but are nonetheless connected to the cerebrospinal fluid that envelops the brain and spinal cord), shows how deeply and in what many-faceted ways this organ is implanted in the human organism.

This stands in great contrast to the eyes, which are enveloped in bony eye-sockets and separated from the rest of the body. The only exceptions are the optic nerve and the central artery and vein of the retina, which provide the only connection through a small region at the back of each eye.

Resources: Husemann (2013); Tortora & Derrickson (2013); Rohen (2007)

Commentary: Sympathy and antipathy

When children relate the story told on the previous day or compare one story to another, their will is activated and permeates their thinking. Whenever the child forms a mental picture, will is involved.

Once we understand the difference between sympathy and antipathy, we can bring this consciousness into our work with the children. For example, if children rush to be first in line to collect the painting paper (an experience of sympathy), we can teach them how to line up according to rows or letters of their names.

By having to listen or think about this, antipathy is stimulated. By becoming conscious, learning to respect others, children develop moral actions.

For example, a child comes to the front of the room to do a math problem. This is an act of will. The child is excited to do the problem and expresses enthusiasm. If the problem is done correctly, the child experiences great sympathy and love. If not, the child experiences antipathy. However, if the child is helped and does the problem again satisfactorily, the antipathy is transformed into a balanced sympathy. When the child looks at the problem in a new way by stepping back and seeing what step was missed, this antipathy helps the child gain a feeling of satisfaction. Antipathy, or the process of stepping back in order to reflect, is necessary in order to think.

Study Questions

1. How does thinking enter into an act of will?
2. How does will enter into thinking?
3. How does our feeling work in relation to our thinking and our will?
4. What is your favorite meditation in Lectures 1 through 5?
5. What is the most important inner activity or exercise for you as a teacher?
6. Find examples of teaching that show great sympathy and enthusiasm in your own work. How does this feeling arise?
7. What is the danger of indiscriminate enthusiasm for everything?
8. Give examples of discerning the demands of the world, of what is required, or needs to be done, in different grades.

Lecture 6
August 27, 1919

Until now we have looked at the human being from the perspective of the soul, since this realm is most accessible to human understanding. Now we need to consider the human being from the standpoint of spirit and only then of body, since we know that the physical is the manifestation of the creative activity of the spiritual and the psychological. From the soul perspective, **sympathy and antipathy** were the key concepts for comprehending the human being. Now we will examine thinking cognition, feeling and willing from the point of view of spirit.

Thinking cognition is experienced as occurring "in the light." The "I" is awake and fully conscious in thinking—for instance in making the judgment that "this person is good." With willing this is not the case. For example, when we walk, we are awake in the *mental picture* [*Vorstellung*] of walking, but not in the *activity* of the bodily organism. In every aspect of our willing there is an element of unconsciousness, even when we think we understand what we are doing (as when we carefully place a beam across two others). Feeling stands halfway between the two. It is partly permeated by consciousness and partly by unconsciousness. Thus we have:

~ Thinking: a wakeful state
~ Willing: a deeply sleeping unconscious state
~ Feeling: a dreaming semi-consciousness (when it is
  experienced rather than *remembered* in wakeful thinking)

While awake, the human being carries all three states of consciousness within him continually, but is fully wakeful only in his thinking cognition. By contrast, as beings of will, we are "asleep" even when we are awake in our thinking.

From the perspective of spirit, in the state of dreamless sleep the entire soul experiences what happens during the daytime in willing, and in the state of dreaming the entire soul experiences what happens during the daytime in feeling. In this sense, we carry all three conditions of waking, dreaming and sleeping through the entire day.

Pedagogically, this knowledge can help us deal with dreamy children, since they live in the feeling realm. In that dreaming tends to awaken after a time, we can approach these children with strong feelings, and these feelings will awaken later as thoughts.

Children who are deeply sleepy—who may even may appear as being retarded—may simply be strong-willed children who are as yet still asleep. As a teacher, one can connect what one wants them to learn with significant activity, such as taking a step for each word in an important sentence. The will, too, will follow the rhythm of sleeping and waking, and awaken one day. Then the child will understand these thoughts. Thus, knowing that the three states of consciousness continually live in us can help us in our pedagogical tasks.

What is the relationship of the "I" to these different states of consciousness? The world around us is permeated by all manner of formative forces, both physical and supra-physical. Think only of the influence that forces of warmth—both physical and metaphysical—have on our surroundings. The "I" cannot as yet be fully aware of them, and so (for its own protection) it is only fully awake in the pictorial reality of thinking cognition. This is the true nature of the mind-body relationship: The "I" is fully awake only in the images created by the physical processes of the body and communicated to the "I" by our thinking cognition.

By contrast, in feeling we do enter at least partially into the actual world but still are unable to endure in full consciousness what is happening, which means the "I" can endure only a dreaming experience of it. The soul would burn up were the "I" able to experience feeling in fully wakened awareness.

We can tolerate what the body undergoes in willing only when consciousness is in the form of deep sleep. The fearful pain of waking in willing would be intolerable.

Thus, in ordinary life the "I" is awake in the images [*Bilder*] of thinking cognition, but only dreamily inspired in mental pictures [*Vorstellungen*] at the level of feeling, which is the source of most artistry. (This inspired experience becomes fully conscious through initiation.) A nightmare is an example of what we would experience if our feeling processes were directly conscious of the processes of ordinary life, in this case the process of air entering and leaving the lung. In willing, we experience unconscious intuitions, which remain inaccessible to our waking consciousness except in auspicious moments. (These intuitions, too, become conscious in initiation.)

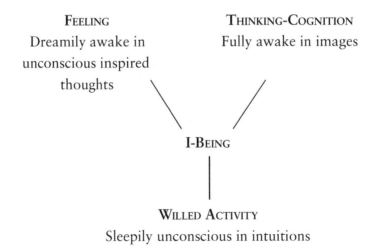

FEELING
Dreamily awake in
unconscious inspired
thoughts

THINKING-COGNITION
Fully awake in images

I-BEING

WILLED ACTIVITY
Sleepily unconscious in intuitions

Poets speak of intuitions, and this is correct, since they draw them forth from their sleeping unconsciousness of will. For example, Goethe was very old when he created Part II of *Faust*; he paced up and down in his study, dictating the lines to his secretary, and this activity of pacing "released" his sleeping intuitions.

People speak of intuitive understanding, but it would be difficult to understand this process if we drew a chart of the life of the "I" in this way –

1. Waking: Pictorial cognition
2. Dreaming: Inspired feeling
3. Sleeping: Intuitive willing

– since this arrangement would obscure the fact that intuitions arise into waking cognition and not into dreaming feelings. A correct drawing needs to show that, whereas what we grasp cognitively sinks down into the body (arrow 1), what emerges from the unconscious realm of willing deep within the body emerges into *cognition* (arrow 2), and not into *feeling*.

This picture can help us understand the form of the human body. The head is separated from the realm of willing so that it can remain still, being carried around by the body like a carriage on the shoulder of porters. This allows the head to be awake in its (inner) activity, while leaving the actual physical willing activity to the lower realms of torso and limbs.

Commentary: Willing, feeling, thinking from the viewpoint of spirit

When we work with dreamy children, we can awaken their thinking by telling stories or describing a situation using strong feelings. Letting children walk while speaking will gradually awaken them. One of the great contributions of craft work is that by the experience of doing, the child's thinking is awakened. This has been referred to as "will-based intelligence."

Study Questions

1. Describe how you can experience being awake in your thinking, asleep in your will and dreaming in your feeling. Relate these to specific activities.

2. How do the first three of the Six Exercises support and strengthen your thinking, willing and feeling? Are they helping you?

3. What is the best approach to awaken a "dreamy" child? What is the best approach to rouse a seemingly "dull" child?

4. Describe an experience you have had of the Ego working in your thinking or your feeling to produce images, mental pictures, or an inking that truth is just around the corner.

5. How is the human being "embedded in the cosmos"?

Lecture 7
August 28, 1919

Steiner again opens by mentioning the course structure and pointing to the methodological approach to the soul via sympathy and antipathy versus the spirit via states of consciousness.

Comprehension is based on relating perceptions to one another [through thinking].[14] Whether those are sense perceptions or soul-spiritual perceptions (i.e., Imagination, Inspiration and Intuitions) as in higher stages of cognition, we must complement them by relating them to one another in time. Thus, we can gain good concepts for body, soul and spirit by looking at the arc of a human lifespan. You will have to develop these concepts further, but we can make a start.

Early in life, the human being is principally body, though the body has to be comprehended also in light of its development into midlife and old age; in midlife the human being is principally soul, and in old age principally spirit. It can happen that a spirit in old age has a body that is no longer flexible enough to allow a person consciousness of its wisdom, but it is wise nonetheless, and in some people this wisdom can become visible well into old age if both body and spirit have retained their elasticity.

In midlife, the human being is principally soul: the realm of freedom. Thus people at this age can even deny the existence of the soul altogether, but in the way that they live in quiet, contemplative states we can recognize a separation of the will from the feeling. Young children, by contrast, have feeling-willing grown together; their actions represent their feelings.

In old age, feeling connects itself and grows together with the opposite pole: thinking. That is why old people come across as wise; they don't spew theories but rather ideas that have been warmed through by the feelings that actual experience allows.

Education must support the separation of feeling from the will, so that feeling can be free to unite with cognition.

We must now consider sensations, which are the first connection we form with the surrounding world. Psychological theories of sensation usually describe a mechanical process outside of us (e.g., vibrations in the air) leading to physiological processes in the sense organs, and them to feelings in the soul. This is useless for understanding the true nature of sensations. We must begin by asking which soul force is most connected with sensation. It is not cognition, as psychologists usually assume.

Sensation has a will nature with a tendency towards feeling. The periphery of the body, the area where the senses are active, is sleeping-dreaming. The sensations enter into us in a dreamy-sleepy manner and are only recognized when wakeful cognition weaves and comprehends them.[15]

Children have will and feeling in their sensation, and that is the reason that we keep emphasizing the use of the will when we teach them. Otherwise we deny their sensation.

In older people sensations connect more with concepts and ideas, since their feeling is connected to cognition. Thus sensation undergoes a change through the course of life, from being connected to the restlessness of will in the child to being connected to cognition in the older person.[16]

The foregoing is an example of learning about the world through actual research and conscious experience, and not just by playing with words. Though the same word, sensation, applies to both young and old, it is a different process depending on the age of the person. Here is an example of learning something through appropriate relating of one observation to another.

The child's sensations originate in the periphery of the body, where sleeping-dreaming lives. Within the body there is another, deeper dreaming-sleeping area (muscles, blood) where the unconscious and subconscious desires live. In between, we are awake only in the nervous system. However, the nervous system has a peculiar connection with the spirit: It shuts itself off, tends to decay, so that the spirit may enter! It is because of the gaps in the nervous system that the spirit-soul can enter. The nerves are the only system in the body that has no direct connection to the spirit. Instead of absorbing the spirit into a living process as the other systems and organs do, the nerves retreat, decay, so the spirit may be revealed. If the nerves were alive, the human being would be asleep. Thus the ordinary picture of the brain and the nerves "thinking" turns reality upside down! In reality they shut off precisely so thinking cognition may unfold.

External stimuli meet the sense organs; there, real (chemical and physical) changes are effected. Such changes also occur in the depths of the body, but between center and periphery the nerves' paths allow the light, tone, etc., to exist again unchanged.

We are awake only in the middle, where the nerves are, and there we live with the external world unhindered by the processes of our physiology. There we *become* light, tone, etc.[17]

Now we must also connect the temporal with sleeping, waking and dreaming.

Remembering and forgetting are akin to waking and sleeping. Remembering is waking a set of images from a state of sleep, while forgetting is putting those same images to sleep.

Here we see that true comprehension comes from observing reality itself. Relating concrete facts such as waking and sleeping to phenomena such as memory brings us to reality rather than to mere words.

Society is becoming more and more decadent around us, as is evident by its reliance on empty words. We have to understand that, because the children we teach belong to this time and are affected by its realities.

Endnotes

14 The Comparative Method: This is one of the most important pedagogical methods developed by Rudolf Steiner in this lecture cycle. He expands upon it in lecture nine, where he explains that a primary goal of Waldorf education is to bring to the students living, mobile concepts that can unfold organically within them as they mature.

For the teacher, the key to this craft is learning to characterize rather than to define. Characterization, Steiner explains, goes beyond mere description; it first receives pulse and life when one phenomenon is compared with another. Taking an example out of the grade school curriculum, he describes in Lecture 9 how "the teacher does not merely describe consecutively... but rather places cuttlefish, mouse and man side-by-side and relates one with another. The interrelationships will prove so manifold that the result will not be a definition but a characterization." In Lecture 7, Rudolf Steiner sets forth this fundamental method in more general terms: "All comprehension is really a question of relating one thing to another: The only way we can comprehend things in the world is by relating them to each other.... We can *comprehend* only if we relate one thing to another in the universe and in our environment."

It is certainly no accident that Rudolf Steiner constructed the foundations of anthroposophy and his own approach to natural science in direct connection with a master practitioner of the *comparative method*: Goethe. In the so-called *Light Course*, Rudolf Steiner describes how "Goethe considered all of that which is known as the natural scientific method to be merely a tool that enables one to group sensory phenomena in such a way that they themselves reveal (speak about) their secrets (GA 320, Lecture 1)." Goethe characterized his approach to nature as *delicate empiricism*. By that he meant a careful attentiveness to the phenomena, a kind of receptive "listening" that silences the premature urge to form an explanatory hypothesis and allows the phenomena to gradually "speak for themselves" (Naydler, 70–71).

Pedagogical Perspectives

One key benefit of the comparative method is how it awakens a sense for gesture when one moves back and forth between the things being compared. For example, take a maple leaf and the needle from a spruce tree. In comparing the two after careful observation we experience how moving from the spruce needle to the expansive, leaf blade of the maple brings a decisive experience of opening up to and interacting with the surrounding light and air. Going from maple leaf to spruce needle, on the other hand, creates the opposite gesture of shrinkage, densification, withdrawal into itself....

A further refinement of this experience can be achieved by creating a mental picture of the first object (after having just observed it directly) and then transforming that image (and its various qualities: density, color, surface texture, etc.) into the second one. Because we construct the first image in our imagination, and no longer with the support of the finished sense perception, we experience how our inner image-building activity must change in moving from one form to the next. We experience the formative gesture that we must produce in order to bring about the transformation—we are becoming aware of our own productive activity as we "recreate in the wake of ever-creating nature" (Goethe). What is being compared plays a huge role in determining which qualities move to the foreground of our experience, but central in all cases is that we move from a static, finished experience of an object to a dynamic one that awakens the sense of something "coming into being"—a sense of formative activity.

This comparative/transformative approach helps us to sense forms and qualities in nature more dynamically. It is helps us move from what Goethe called the *Gestalt* to another level of experience that he referred to as *Bildung*:

> The Germans have a word for the complex of existence presented by a physical organism: *Gestalt* (structured form). With this expression they exclude what is changeable and assume that an interrelated whole is identified, defined and fixed in character. But if we look at all these Gestalten, especially the organic ones, we will discover that nothing in them is permanent, nothing is at rest or defined—everything is in a flux of continual motion. This is why German frequently and fittingly makes use of the word *Bildung* (formation) to describe the end product and what is in process of production as well. Thus in setting forth a morphology we should not speak of Gestalt, or if we use the term we should at least do so only in reference to the idea, the concept, or to an empirical element held fast for a mere moment of time. When something has acquired a form it metamorphoses immediately to a new one. If we wish to arrive at some living perception of Nature we ourselves must remain as quick and flexible as Nature and follow the example she gives. (Goethe, in Miller 1988, pp. 63–64)

In contrast to static definitions that "fix or mark the limits of" a few identifying traits unique to what is being considered, the comparative (transformative) approach steps across those isolating boundaries and helps awaken process-related experiences that, instead of fixing (*Gestalt*), reveal gesture and formative tendencies (*Bildung*).

Comparisons are open-ended, they are "conversations" between the phenomena being compared, and each conversation is unique to those particular conversing partners. When compared to an oak, a maple will "speak" somewhat differently to us than when it is contrasted with a beech, or a rose bush. A spruce will "speak" in more subtle tones when transformed (in our imagination) into a fir tree rather than a birch.

The possibilities of comparison are endless, they are only limited by the time and energy we are willing to invest in providing the opportunity for various organisms to speak of themselves and each other upon the inner stage of our comparison-capable consciousness.

Resources: Goethe (1988); Grohmann (1996); Holdrege (2009); Julius (1969); Margulis & Sagan (2000); Naydler (1996)

15 Perceptions without the input of thinking are sleepy/ dreamy in nature: From a purely philosophical/epistemological perspective, the sleepy/dreamy nature of our not-yet-thinking-permeated perceptions can also be confirmed. The 25-year-old Rudolf Steiner, in his first book *The Science of Knowing* (1886), formulated the matter as follows:

> Let us now take a look at pure experience. What does it contain, as it sweeps across our consciousness, without our working upon it in thinking? It is mere juxtaposition in space and succession in time; an aggregate of utterly disconnected particulars. None of the objects that come and go there has anything to do with any other. At this stage, the facts that we perceive, that we experience inwardly, are of no consequence

to each other. This world is a manifoldness of things of equal value. No thing or event can claim to play a greater role in the functioning of the world than any other part of the world of experience. If it is to become clear to us that this or that fact has greater significance than another one, we must then not merely observe the things, but must already bring them into thought-relationships... After the activation of our thinking, each particular of this total picture no longer appears in the way our senses alone communicate it, but already with the significance it has for the whole of reality. It appears then with characteristics totally lacking to it in the form of experience. (pp. 24–26)

This topic is not just of interest to students of philosophy or anthroposophy, however. It is pivotal in a profound revolution regarding the formative role that thinking plays in modern science that took place mid-20th century. Central in this paradigm shift was the approach of Yale philosophy professor N.R. Hanson. With his often-quoted words that "there is more to seeing than meets the eye," Hanson encapsulates a central theme in his analysis of the nature of perception. When discussing something like a hexagon with diagonals, for example, he asks if all individuals who see this figure—and who, if they are requested to, are able to produce essentially identical drawings of this figure—actually see the same thing?

Hexagon with Diagonals (after Goebel, 1982)

Although the tiny inverted images on each viewer's retina will be virtually the same, some will see a hexagon with diagonals, others the point of a crystal, yet others will see in it a cube viewed from above, and still others a cube seen from below. A fourth group might only see lines crisscrossing in a plane, and so on. Although nothing essential changes at the level of optics or physiology—people see different things! What changes is not the sensory data as such, but the *organization of what one sees*. Organization is not an element in the visual field, it is brought to the raw material of perception by our thinking. Similarly, Hanson points out, the plot is not another detail in a story, nor is the melody merely one more note in a song. Yet in the absence of plots and melodies, the elements of a story and the notes of a song would not hang together. As Rudolf Steiner suggests in this lecture, they would remain only "dreamy" sense impressions that have not yet been organized into a clear and wakeful perceptual whole. Indeed, "there is more to seeing than meets the eye."

Resources: Holdrege (2009); Hanson (1958); Steiner (1886, 1988)

16 The feeling-willing nature of children's perception:
How the living, imaginative, with feeling- and will-permeated way in which young children perceive the world begins to fade as they grow older is beautifully described by Herman Hesse in his *Autobiographical Writings*:

> I did not want to leave my world where things were good and precious. There was, to be sure, a completely secret goal for me when I thought about the future. The only thing I ardently wished for was to become a magician. This wishful dream remained true to me for a long time, but eventually it began to lose its omnipotence.... Slowly, slowly, the blossom withered,

slowly out of the unlimited, something limited was coming toward me, the real world, the world of grownups.... Already the infinite, many-splendored world of the possible was limited for me, divided into fields, cut up by fences. Gradually the primeval forest of my days was altered, paradise congealed around me. I no longer remained what I was, prince and king in the land of the possible. I was not becoming a magician. I was learning Greek, in two years Hebrew would be added.... Imperceptibly this contraction took place, perceptibly the magic faded around me. The marvelous story in my grandfather's book was still beautiful, but it was on a certain page whose number I knew and it was there today and tomorrow and at every hour, there was no further miracle.... I was surrounded by disenchantment on every hand, much became narrow that once had been open, much became tawdry that once had been golden. (pp. 21–22)

17   The Nerves as "empty spaces" for the spirit and soul:

As was explained in Endnote 5, Lecture 2, the pathways of much of the human nervous system are lined with strongly materialized, crystal-like lipid deposits known as myelin. They represent the counter-pole to the ongoing renewal and transformation through cell division and differentiation that constantly takes place in most of the organism. In order to better understand this, it is important to realize how—based on outer perception—we normally put a one-sided emphasis on the finished forms of the body. In contrast to this illusion of the human being as made primarily up of "solid" organs, Rudolf Steiner points out that:

The outer spatial forms of human organs are merely living processes that have come to a "standstill" for a moment. In reality, organs such as the lungs, stomach, heart, liver and kidneys are not that which they appear to be at first glance: as clearly circumscribed, quiescent forms. No these organs only give the illusion of such solidly and constancy, for in reality they are in constant living movement, they are not finished, completed forms, but living processes. We should speak of the heart process, the lung processes, kidney processes, etc. (GA 53, cited in Selg, 2000, p. 488; trans. MH)

With this more dynamic understanding of an organism, we can better grasp what Steiner is saying when he refers to the soul-spiritual forces being absorbed—being constantly engaged, "put to work"—in the growth, developmental and maintenance processes of the living organism. Only in the counter-pole—in the death and matter deposition processes of the mineralizing nervous system—are those forces no longer engaged, but freed (emancipated) and thus accessible for conscious experience.

Resources: See Endnote 5, Lecture 2; Selg (2000, p. 488)

Commentary: Children have the soul forces of feeling and willing together.

Working through the senses strengthens the connection between them. Gradually over the primary school years, feeling is separated from willing and is connected with thinking. Brain research tells us that the feelings connected with learning a particular skill arise every time that skill is practiced. For example, if a child felt fear when learning division, every time he/she approaches a division problem, the feeling of fear is aroused and blocks continued learning. When children learn with joy, they are able to build skills more effectively.

Rather than having students memorize a concept, the teacher strengthens comprehension by having the children relating one thing to another.

Study Questions

1. Describe the process by which we as human beings come to know the world through observation/perception, reflection and concept.

2. Contrast how this process works differently in two children you know.

3. Create a drawing or poem or scene inspired by the thought that in childhood the human being is predominantly physical, in middle age predominantly soul, and in old age predominantly spiritual.

4. How do we work in education to free the feeling of the child from his/her will? Why is this necessary?

5. How do we work to make the child's environment a "true experience" of the world? What in the modern environment "contradicts" the child's sense experience?

6. How do you employ the rhythm of learning-forgetting-remembering in your teaching? Why is this healthy for the children?

Lecture 8
August 29, 1919

Our pedagogical goal in the course is to bring the unknown closer to the known, and our method is to relate obscure processes such as remembering and forgetting to more observable processes such as sleeping and waking.

We know from experience that sleep is important for the proper functioning of our "I," our consciousness. When our sleep is disturbed by external influences (e.g., mosquitoes), we become more irritable, more sensitive, and our consciousness becomes weaker the next day.

Something similar is true regarding the regulation of remembering and forgetting. Daydreaming is an example of a state in which images from the surrounding world enter into consciousness without the will being involved and swoosh around willy-nilly. A daydreamer is not making an effort to learn something about the surrounding world, neglecting to involve the "I" in a proper relationship with the environment. This is, of course, especially typical of a child.

We can help bring memory processes into the will, i.e., the act of remembering, by first recognizing the will's role in them. The will brings about memory by raising images from the unconscious into consciousness. By raising children to have healthy habits in body, soul and spirit, we can support the will indirectly, since (because it is asleep) we cannot influence it directly. If our methods of instruction awaken lively interest in the children, then the will is engaged and strengthened and their memory will be stronger. Contrary to memorization methods, a healthy pedagogy influences the memory by awakening strong feelings and thereby strengthening the will.

This is again an example of how we must study the human being, both as a differentiated three-fold being of thinking, feeling and willing and as a unified being in which the three parts are present in one another and do not exist in isolation. What is cognitive is only mainly cognitive, and has feeling and willing in it, and so forth. Focusing only on abstract unity makes everything gray; focusing only on the separate parts precludes understanding of the whole.

We can now apply this notion to the realm of the senses, maintaining an inner flexibility in the face of seeming contradictions that are inevitable when studying the human being.

The human being has twelve senses.[18] The more obvious ones are recognized because of their specific organs; the others go unrecognized because their organs are less distinctly formed.

The perception of another person's "I" is based on a sense, though it does not have an organ like an eye or ear. It is spread over the whole body and composed of a very fine substance. When we meet another person, there is a rapid vibration of sympathy (flowing into the other) and antipathy (retreating into ourselves as though under attack). In this case sympathy and antipathy are not meant in the sense of feeling but as the process of perceiving another. This process is, at the same time, an alternation between sleeping and waking. The "I"- sense goes into the other person in a sleeping-will activity, then retreats and brings the impression it has formed back into a waking-cognitive process. We are asleep in the other, but wake up to the other in ourselves. This is so rapid that we do not notice it, but it is how we perceive the "I" of another. The first appendix of "Intuitive Thinking as a Spiritual Path" describes this process in more detail.

A second cognitive sense is for the thoughts of another person, which we again perceive directly before understanding it and can perceive not only in words but in gestures and so on. Speech is perceived through yet a third cognitive sense.

There are, further, the senses of hearing, temperature, sight, taste and smell. Then there is a sense of balance, through which we maintain our uprightness without falling, and a sense of (our own) movement, through which we feel the movement or stillness of our body. There is also the sense of life, through which we feel the condition of our body (hunger, level of energy, comfort). Thus there are twelve senses in all.

The senses can be grouped thus:

Will Senses: touch, life, movement and balance
Feeling Senses: smell, taste, sight and temperature

The sense of sight only gives us color. We gain cognizance of a round colored shape by utilizing our sense of movement to perform the circular motion within ourselves super-sensibly, and then together with the color added by the sense of sight, we perceive a round colored form. This is an example of how the world presents itself to us in twelve ways, through twelve senses, and how our judgment unites the disparate sensory impressions into comprehensive perceptions. It is, therefore, crucially important to develop all twelve senses properly in education.

Then there are the

Cognitive Senses: "I," thought, speech and hearing.

Thus we see how will, feeling and cognition live in the region of the human "I" and can affect the spirit through the states of waking, sleeping and dreaming. The soul aspect is affected

83

through (and comprehended by considering) sympathy and antipathy, and, as we shall see, the physical aspects of thinking, feeling and will are comprehended by considering the forms of the body.

Endnotes

18   The Twelve Senses: The twelve senses are a very large and central topic in anthroposophy and Waldorf education. Rudolf Steiner spoke about the various human senses in many different lectures over the course of more than twenty years. The foundation for this was originally presented in his book, *Anthroposophy (A Fragment)*. There is also a considerable literature to this theme by other anthroposophical authors. Three good starting points available in English would be:

> ~ Aeppli, W. (1996). *The Care and Development of the Human Senses*
> ~ Schoorel, E. (2004). *The First Seven Years: Physiology of Childhood*
> ~ Soesman, A. (1990). *Our Twelve Senses*

Very lively descriptions of the functioning (or malfunctioning) of several human senses can also be found in the well-known book by Oliver Sacks, *The Man Who Mistook His Wife for a Hat*.

Commentary: The twelve senses

Because the will is asleep, the teacher cannot give a child direct training in the use of his will, but we can help develop habits in his soul, body and spirit that lead to an exertion of the will on particular occasions.

Awakening a vivid interest in the subject increases interest and affects the child's will. Then the mental pictures of the subject, e.g., animals, will be brought forward from the subconscious, from the area of forgetting. When the teacher frames a rich mental picture, the child can step into it and experience it. The power of memory must be derived from the feeling and will and not from mere intellectual memory exercises.

The key principle is from unity to differentiation and then unity, or as it is often said, "From the whole to the parts to the whole."

Steiner introduces the twelve senses as a foundation for understanding the child's relationship to self and the world. The will senses—touch, life, movement, balance—are the basis of the young child's experience and for healthy brain development from birth onwards. Early childhood and kindergarten teachers emphasize these senses as they are fundamental to the development of the higher senses—hearing speech, thought and ego. The feelings are activated through the senses of smell, taste, sight and warmth. Adults model the higher senses for children, but as they get older, they can directly experience the world through the higher senses.

Because the child does not yet work out of the ego, the teacher is the representative of an ego being, modeling behaviors and attitudes that the child will first imitate and later form out of him/herself.

The twelve senses are like twelve different windows through which we experience the world. When we experience them separately, we bring them together in ourselves and are able to make judgments and form concepts.

Study Questions

1. How does healthy sleep support a child's learning and memory?
2. What can you do to help children strengthen their will?

3. What can you do to help children strengthen their memory?
4. How do the four lower (or foundational) senses transform into the four highest senses in the human being? (Hint: Think from physical to spiritual and from inner to outer).
5. Which of the twelve senses are now recognized by modern science? Draw correlations.
6. Share good practices for conducting a morning review (or recall) with the children at various ages.

Lecture 9
August 30, 1919

A deep understanding of human development, when permeated by feeling and will, will awaken a pedagogical instinct in you that will allow you to teach well. The knowledge base must be genuine, however, and for this we must build a comprehensive view from the perspectives of spirit (stages of consciousness), soul, and finally the bodily aspect as well. Then we shall reach a discussion of what is a health-giving pedagogy.

We must remember that the first two decades of life are divided into three seven-year phases: Before the change of teeth the child is an imitative being; between seven and puberty the child yearns to follow an authority, and the wish for independent judgment arises only after puberty. Therefore, during the grade school years we have to teach out of the principle of authority. However, as teachers we must also understand what the acquisition of logic entails, even if our knowledge remains in the background when we teach. We must carry the essentials of logic within us.

Acting logically always consists of three parts. First of all we form conclusions. This is the most conscious part of logic, and all speech is permeated with conclusions. Theoretical logic dissects conclusions artificially and thereby misses what actually happens in life. In reality, when confronted with a new perception (e.g., a lion), we embed it in the context of our life heretofore, and that is a conclusion. Then we compare it and place it into our previous scope of knowledge, and that is a judgment (e.g., "the lion is an animal"). Finally, we form the individual concept "lion" that theoretical logic usually considers the first step. But because our life does not begin when we see the lion, we first bring the lion into our previous experience and knowledge and, in turn, then add it to this sum of knowledge as the newly acquired concept. First, the lion is a conclusion; then it is a judgment and finally a concept. We are not aware that this process is going on within us, but it is nonetheless.

The classic syllogism (all people are mortal; John is a person; therefore John is mortal) takes three judgments and artificially makes them into a process. In reality you have all three of these judgments upon first meeting "John," then you consciously arrive at the third one, and finally you form the concept "the mortal John."

How do these three elements (conclusion, judgment, concept) behave in the human spirit? Conclusions are only healthy when they live in the fully wakeful, conscious life. It is therefore ruinous to children to have them memorize finished conclusions. When you receive students who have been taught many dead conclusions, you do not want to have them retrieve those, but instead allow them to form conclusions anew.

Judgments are formed in full consciousness, but then trickle down into the dreaming soul. Conclusions should not trickle there, but judgment should. The dreaming soul is the realm of feeling, and what trickles down into feeling becomes the habit life. We therefore educate the children's habit life in the way we demonstrate to them, through our speaking, how to form judgments.

Concepts descend into the sleeping soul, and there work right into the formation of the physical body. Although only refining what nature had already produced through inheritance from the parents, the concepts taught children do in fact act on the body to an extent discernible in the features of adults.

The blandness and uniformity of people in our time are testaments to the bad education they received as children.

Concepts can live in the unconscious; judgments live in the semi-conscious as habits; conclusions should only live in the fully conscious. This means that we should not provide the children with finished conclusions, but instead with conclusions that can ripen into flexible, growing concepts as the children mature and layer additional experiences into richer textures. We can do that by avoiding definitions and characterizing life from a multiplicity of perspectives, relating them one to the other. Thus, a squid, a mouse, and a human being should not be defined in isolation, but characterized and related to one another.

Fixed concepts that do not need to change can provide the child with a framework in the soul, but the details of life must be taught so they can grow organically with the child. Especially important is to relate everything to the human being, so that both nature and human ingenuity (e.g., the telegraph) are facets of a comprehensive picture of the human being. A multi-faceted, rich concept of the human being is the most beautiful thing a child can take from a healthy schooling.

When we educate children to a healthy, honoring, respectful approach to life, when, that is, we imbue the teaching with a prayerful attitude in the most encompassing sense, we sow seeds in their souls that can grow and metamorphose into the capacity to bless in old age.

We can now look at the three phases of childhood through a different lens. When children come into the world, they bring with them an assumption that this world is like the spiritual world whence they came. Therefore, they are willing to imitate their surroundings and assume that the world is moral, that it is good. The young child is oriented toward the past in the spiritual world and assumes that the world is good.

During the grade-school years, the child yearns to live in the present. We should teach in such a way that the present might be enjoyed, but not enjoyed superficially. Rather, the teacher should be imbued with the artistic, with an approach that finds beauty in the world above anything mundane and pedantic. It is useless to give teachers manuals [!!!]. Every teacher must draw upon his or her own relationship to art in finding tasteful things to bring the students.

Only after puberty is a systematic quality appropriate, for then the student yearns to find truth, rather than beauty or goodness, as the fundamental quality in the world. The adolescent is future oriented, beginning to develop the impulses that will lead into the future, and truth is the quality most suited for that phase.

Commentary: From the viewpoint of the body: Conclusion, judgment, concept

The teacher needs to understand the growing child, especially the nature of will. In the child's first seven years, the child imitates the teacher. In the primary school, the child longs to follow the authority of the teacher in thinking, feeling and willing. From puberty onwards, students want to form their own individual judgment about the world.

The teacher has to hold his or her own authority during the primary school years. This is a loving authority, not an authoritarian approach. Over time this changes and the child begins to question the adult's authority and form independent judgment.

The facts of the child's experience make up the world of conclusions. This will depend on what the child has been exposed to previously. Based on these conclusions the child considers a new sense perception and weighs it in order to come to a concept. Steiner gives the example of a lion. Children are most awake in their conclusions.

For example: My family did not have an automobile. When I was 12, I repeatedly observed license plates on the backs of cars. The year 1950 was on the plates. I came to the concept that the year referred to how old the car was. However, my perception showed that new cars and old cars had the same year on the plate. I could not come to a correct concept because I lacked the experience of knowing that license plates had to be registered every year.

A city child has different conclusions than a country child. For example, going to buy milk in a bottle or container in a food market. The country child knows the milk came from a cow, but the city child may think it comes from the container. Children in different communities have their own conclusions based on their life experiences.

"The conclusion is only healthy when it occurs fully in waking life." When the child is able to bring experience to conclusions, he/she is awake and has mental pictures of the object. From this, the child can make healthy judgments and come to a concept. Children growing up in different cultures bring very different mental pictures to their judgments and thus concept. This is important in understanding how children develop biases against people who are different from them.

"When we form a concept it goes down into the profoundest depth of man's being, into the sleeping soul." This is the reason it is so difficult to change a child's perception once early concepts have been accepted.

The teacher needs to be aware that he/she is adding judgments to the children's soul life. This is a powerful reality. The teacher is able to help children find a positive relationship

91

to their society, to the world, through conscious statements. For example, if a teacher states that global warming does not exist, the children will ignore opportunities to care for the environment. If the teacher says it exists but we cannot do anything about it, the child's soul can feel helpless and lamed. If the teacher says global warming does exist and there is much we can do about it, the child's will, feeling and thinking are activated with a sense of purpose. Of course, the age of the child is significant for how the teacher brings judgment as a conclusion.

Another example: If the teacher brings the class to an awakened consciousness of being part of a school community, the children will relate to other classes in a positive way. If the teacher emphasizes the individual class as a separate unity, the children will more likely isolate themselves from other classes.

"The teacher should give living concepts that children can change in later life. Definitions are dead concepts. Give characterizations instead." This is a basic pedagogical direction which Rudolf Steiner gave to the teachers. It is different from the intellectual approach which gives finished concepts. By characterizing, showing different views of a subject, the child develops his/her own concept, which can change with more experience. It is not a fixed concept.

For example, in 7th grade Renaissance explorations study, the teacher can present the view of a European explorer meeting Africans for the first time and an African meeting a European for the first time. Similarly with explorations to North America. The child forms a different concept by experiencing different views than the one-sided view expressed in some literature.

Connect everything with the human being. By doing this, the child comes to an experience of the human being within nature, within society and within a higher order. In 6th grade physics the connection can be made between sound in nature, through different materials, air and water, and how the human being experiences sound. This can lead to an understanding of deafness and sign language, relating the child to other human beings.

Give the child concepts of reverence and devotion that are open to change. This awakens the child to a sense of morality and ideals.

Steiner concludes this lecture with the goals of education at different stages of a child's life:

Birth to seven: enjoyment and sense of goodness
Seven to fourteen: The world is beautiful.
Fourteen through high school years: The world is true.

This understanding supports the stages of child development and guides the teacher in approaching children of different ages.

Study Questions

1. Why are definitions and ready-made conclusions detrimental to the development of the child?
2. Observe a plant. Try to characterize it without defining it.
3. Create an image or metaphor for a process in nature.
4. How do goodness, beauty and truth relate to the three 7-year stages of child development?

Lecture 10
September 1, 1919

The three aspects of the human body have different forms.

~ *The Head* is a sphere that is completely sense perceptible.

~ *The Chest* is a crescent-moon shape that visibly manifests only part of a larger sphere. The back of the sphere shows, but the front blends into a soul state and remains invisible.

~ *The Limbs* are the radii of a sphere. These radii are inserted into the trunk.[19]

As mentioned before, we will gain a lively image of the subject only by relating the parts together. Thus the limb nature of the human being is primarily present in the limbs, but the head also has stunted "limbs:" the jawbones. The true limbs are essentially blood and muscles, will vehicles, with bones for support. The head's "limbs" are related to the head's principle task (intelligence) and are therefore bonier.[20]

We see how outer forms reveal inner aspects.

The relationship of the tubular limb bones to the bowl-like bones of the head is a very difficult one to grasp, but one that we must grapple with.

When Goethe observed a sheep's skull, he perceived that it is a transformed vertebra. This is a simple imaginative exercise to understand, since with a little pushing and pulling on parts of the vertebra we can arrive at a skull bone.[21] It is more difficult to see the tubular bones as a transformation of the skull, because that relationship is not simply an enlargement or reduction of one part or another. Rather, the limb bones have be turned inside out in order to arrive at the shape of the skull bones. The limb bones are not just a transformation of the skull bones, but the skull bones turned inside out.

The head has its center inside, in a point. The center of the partially visible sphere of the chest lies outside of the body, in the distance. The limbs' center is actually a sphere that is the whole periphery; the center of the limbs is the opposite of the point inside the head. [These statements about the limbs' center can only be understood with the help of projective geometry.]

What arises in the head has its origin inside of us. With the limbs, however, we are connected to the whole periphery; the world is inserted into us, as it were. Only a tiny portion of the limb system becomes visible. Spiritually, the limbs are connected to the whole universe.

So we can also view the human being as three circles: The head is entirely visible, the chest is partially visible, and with the limbs we see only a small portion of the radii of the largest circle.[22]

In the central area, we see the interaction of the head and limbs in the formation of the ribcage. Towards the back, the ribcage is closed; towards the front, it manages closure when near the head, but then grows increasingly limb-like, open, as we move downwards.

In the ancient sculptures of the Egyptians, and especially the Greeks, there is expression of their understanding that the human being is connected with the whole universe.

From was said already, we see that the head is inclined inward, while the limbs are inclined outward. In truth, the limbs are inclined towards the cosmos, and when we move, they relate to the movements of the cosmos. The head, by contrast, has to rest on the shoulders. It has to bring to inner stillness the movements of the cosmos.

What do our limbs do when they imitate the cosmos? They dance! True dance is an expression of cosmic movements. The head and chest cannot do that; they make the soul reflect on the movements of the limbs. When we move irregularly, the soul growls; when we move rhythmically, the soul murmurs; when we dance in harmony with the universe, the soul makes song (outwardly) and music (inwardly).

Understanding that what we express outwardly in movement comes to rest within us and is then transformed into tone is a key to a true comprehension of sense perception. The organs of perception do not participate in the movement, but reflect them downwards into the chest, and there they become music and color. The arts are the movements "digested" by the sense organs and the chest.

In modern education, a lack of understanding for these difficult concepts leads to an incomplete understanding of the human being. Only the outside is understood, which is like knowing only about the outside of a glove. The limbs, for example, are not understood at all because they are spirit turned inside out, but the spirit isn't seen.

This threefold picture can be seen in another way as well: The whole human being standing before us as a limb being (the large sphere) is composed of body, soul and spirit. As a chest being (middle sphere), the human being is a being of body and soul. As a head being (smallest sphere): body only. When the Catholic Church declared in 869 that the human being is a being of body and soul only, the connection of the human being with the cosmos was driven out of the realm of knowledge, paving the way to increasing egotism in religion and to scientific materialism.

For example, let's look at the human head. Now the head is actually descended from the animal world, and science rightly connects us with the animal kingdom as regards our head.[23] But the chest was added later and is less connected with animalistic tendencies; the limbs came last and are not descended from the animals at all.[24] But because the church wanted to hide the spiritual connection of the human being with the cosmos, later ages could focus only on those aspects that are descended from the animal world, and today believe that everything about the human being has its origin in animal existence.[25]

Today we arrived at an overarching historical theme by taking our starting point in the sphere, the crescent and the radii. It is very important for the teacher to understand the origins of the cultural realities of the present. Correct thoughts about the nature of the children before us make a crucial difference to the way we teach. When we replace the notion of the animalistic origin of humanity with one that sees the connection of the children with the cosmos, we can appreciate that rather than training young animals to become like us, we are meeting individuals who connect with the entire universe. The classroom becomes a center of cosmic activity!

If we take the concepts developed today and cultivate the appropriate feeling from them, then we become one with our students. Subtle connections form between the students and teachers, similar to the way that the earth itself conducts electricity between wires attached to copper plates.

Endnotes

19 Limbs as radii inserted into the trunk

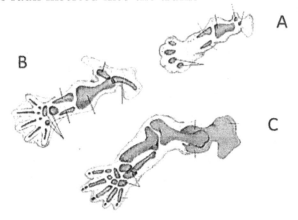

Embryological Development of a Human Limb (After Sadler, 2000.)

A. Lower extremity of an early six week embryo showing the first hyaline cartilage formation.

B. At the end of the sixth week.

C. At the end of eighth week.

The three stages of limb formation shown above speak for themselves. Particularly striking is the insertive gesture from the outside-in found in the knee/elbow and hip/shoulder joints.

Resource: Sadler (2000)

20 The Limbs of the Head: In the arms and legs—our organs of movement—the radial principle dominates. In the head, however—where spherical, plate-like bones and fixed bone connections rule—the organs of movement, the jaws, have changed dramatically. In the realm of the head forces they have shrunk in size and are no longer embedded in muscle. The upper jaw has fused—as things in the head usually do—with the head bones adjacent to it and has lost all mobility, thereby providing passive opposition to the active pressure of the lower jaw. Whereas our powerful, gravity overcoming thigh bones are embedded in massive muscles and no longer accessible to direct touch, the jaw bones can be felt from ear to chin. Whereas our trunk limbs consist of tubular bones, the jaws, in correspondence with their environment, have become flat and more surface-like.

Although the lower jaw is still connected to powerful, mastication-enabling jaw muscles (masseter, etc.), both jaws are also surrounded by something new—a fine network of muscles that do not cause movement around a joint (radial movement), but move the skin! These are the muscles of facial expression (depressor anguli oris, etc.). These muscles no longer serve the activity of the will in the realm of gravity, but—in their much-reduced form—the communication of our inner life. What's more, with the help of these and the tongue muscles (genioglossus, etc.) the region between the jaw-limbs also becomes a space for the articulation of human speech.

So we see that the limb region of the human head not only serves

~ as the beginning of the digestive system through the chewing activity of the jaws,
~ but also as a disclosure of our inner feeling life through facial expression muscles, and
~ for the articulation of our thoughts and experiences through the spoken word.

Resources: Leber (2002); Chung & Chung (2012)

21 Vertebrae metamorphose to head bones: Rudolf Steiner provides a simple picture of how one might imagine this transformation in a lecture on January 4, 1915 (CW 275).

Goethe himself relates that one day when he was going for a walk in the Jewish cemetery in Venice he found a sheep's skull that had fallen apart at the seams. Picking it up and looking at the form of the bones the thought occurred to him, 'When I look at these head bones, what actually are they? They are transformed dorsal vertebrae.'

You know, of course, that the spinal cord that encloses the spine marrow as a nerve cord is composed of rings which fit into one another, rings with a definite shape and processes (procesus vertebralis). And if you imagine one of these rings expanding so that the hole the marrow passes through—for the rings fit into one another—begins to get larger and the bone gets correspondingly thinner and expands like elastic, not only in a horizontal direction but also in other directions, then the form that arises out of this ring form is nothing else but the bone formation which forms our skullcap. Our skullcaps are transformed dorsal vertebrae.

22 Limbs as Radii: In this lecture Rudolf Steiner describes the head as a sphere with its center within that goes through a transformation (with the torso as a transition phase), the result of which is the formation of the limbs as the visible ends of radii coming from a sphere whose midpoint is everywhere in the periphery! This less than obvious statement can be pictured more easily with the help of a radii-imbued sphere that expands gradually until turning inside out, whereby the radii then ray in from the periphery.

23 Human head evolved from animals: Although this topic is too large to explore in the current context, it is interesting to see how Rudolf Steiner touches upon the evolution of the human head in his lectures to doctors (*Spiritual Science and Medicine*, Lecture III, 23 Mar. 1920), where he notes that:

> ...even a superficial observation of the human head with its various enclosed nerve centers, reminds one rather of lower forms than highly developed species of animal life, in that the nerve centers are enclosed in a firm armor of bone. The human head actually reminds us of prehistoric animals. It is only somewhat transformed. And if we describe the lower animal forms, we generally do so by referring to their external skeleton, whereas the higher animals and man have their bony structure inside. Nevertheless our head, our most highly evolved and specialized part, has an external skeleton.

Steiner also refers to the human head in relation to the molluscs—in particular the squid (cuttlefish) in *Practical Advice to Teachers*, Lecture 7 (pp. 104–109). Mollusks typically secrete an external shell, which forms an exoskeleton that surrounds the soft internal tissues of the animal, reminiscent of how human cranial bones surround the brain.

24 Human Uprightness: An Evolutionary Game-Changer: For many years two schools of thought argued about which came first in human (Hominid) evolution, larger brains or bipedalism (upright stance and gait). In recent decades fossils unearthed by anthropologists have settled that debate. These fossils show that bipedalism clearly preceded larger brain development, with knee joint, ankle, pelvic and leg bones, as well as foot prints, demonstrating the existence of uprightness at a time when human brains were no larger than those of apes and less than half the size of a modern *Homo sapiens* brain. The shape of the head—with its pronounced jaw and receding forehead—also bore animal-like traits at that time.

Just as in animals, where we find that different organs are emphasized in the various species, in humans the organs of uprightness dominate. They allow us to be centered in ourselves, in contrast to the environment-oriented horizontality of the animal. Upright posture requires constant will activity, balancing between forward and backward, right and left through continuous compensating movements. Through maintaining this balance we experience ourselves in our centeredness. Our entire body reveals the signature of the vertical. Our unusually long legs represent an enormous growth against gravity from childhood to puberty and are connected with characteristic morphological and functional changes, such as:

~ The formation of the arch of the foot
~ Strong development of the big toe
~ Massive lower thoracic and lumbar vertebrae
~ Deep integration of the spine into the chest
~ Long neck relative to the primates
~ Large mastoid process at the base of the skull
~ Wide and flattened form of the rib cage
~ Shift of the shoulder blades into the back and the torsion of the humerus—which permits free movement of hands and arms within the field of vision

The development of all these organs goes beyond what they attain in higher animals. Eventually, this uprightness leads to the human form of the head as well—among other things, the forehead develops and the frontal brain behind it. This part of the brain is central to the characteristically human activities of planning and forethought, concentration and logical thinking—all of which allow us to move from awareness to self-awareness and to the development of "I" consciousness.

Resources: Kranich (1999); Larsen, Matter & Gebo (1998); Losos, Mason et al. (2016); Verhulst (2003)

25 869 and Scientific Materialism: Rudolf Steiner's statement that the banishment of the spirit by the Catholic Church in 869 is a primary factor leading to scientific materialism may seem rather surprising. As described in Endnote 10 (Lecture 3), however, the removal of the individual human spirit from the trinity of body, soul and spirit had significant implications. As natural scientists began to explore the fossil record, and to discover there a kind of "evolutionary (phylogenetic) tree," whose branches appeared to show *evolutionary* relationships among various biological species, finding a plausible explanation for such patterns became the highest of priorities. Without a concept of the individual human spirit as distinct from the animal world available to it, the field of scientific explanation was left uncontested to a purely physical form of causality based on pure chance.

Commentary: The body

This lecture is directed to the teacher to perceive the threefold aspect of the body—the head, chest and limbs. The diagram is helpful to grasp the different forms (head – round, sunlike; chest – a fragment of a sphere, moon form; and limbs – radii of a sphere related to the universe).

Each part of the body is also experienced in the other parts. For example, in the face, the bones of the upper and lower jaws are stunted limbs.

In my opinion, now comes one of the most difficult part in all these lectures—metamorphosis. Steiner calls on Goethe's observations of the skull. At first it is difficult to grasp what is being stated, but through sculpture and exercises in imagination we may be able to make progress.

The description of the head bringing to rest what the limbs perform in movement leads to our understanding of the change the child goes through in first grade. Instead of imitating movement outside, the child begins to create mental pictures of movement within the soul. A child who cannot do this cannot sit still but is constantly in movement.

In this lecture the connection between the musical arts and the plastic arts is made. The plastic arts are outside the child and move into the child's soul (sculpting, forms of building). In the musical arts the child takes in the impressions from the plastic arts and moves from within out into the world (singing, playing an instrument). Some movements within the soul are barely perceived consciously. For example, we perceive a color and something resonates within. Different colors will cause different inner movements. This is the subject of art therapy.

In many lectures, Rudolf Steiner refers to the year 869 in which the Catholic Church denies the threefoldness of the human being in relation to the spirit. By referring to the human being as body and soul (with a little spirit), the individual human being has been separated from the world of spirit and has to rely on others for spiritual guidance. This leads to the current prevalent materialistic view.

A deep sense of reverence is evoked with the statement that "What I do with the growing child has significance for the whole universe." Teachers living with this thought fill their soul with a sense of holiness. It makes our daily work purposeful and filled with meaning. This attitude of reverence passes as an underground current between the teacher and the child. In holding the feeling that we are part of the great universe, the teacher brings the art of education alive.

Study Questions

1. Give an example of how the form of the human body reveals its inner nature.
2. Describe how we can see the threefold structure of the human body within each realm: head, trunk and limbs.
3. Draw or sculpt a series of human vertebrae and discuss the process of metamorphosis in the series.
4. Turn a sock inside out, and use it to explain the polarity of head and limb.
5. Describe how the movement and music of the world enters into the human being.
6. How does music arise within the human being? Compare this to how memory and concept arise. (Lecture 2)
7. Give an example of how you use the "subconscious stream" of thought with children in the classroom.

Lecture 11
September 2, 1919

In Lecture 10 we saw that the head is primarily physical, the chest has physical and soul characteristics, and the limbs have physical, soul and spiritual characteristics.

Looked at a different way, the head can be said to have relatively complete physical form at birth, with a dreaming soul and a sleeping spirit. The physical form, having gone through the animal stages earlier in evolution, is more or less complete. Up until the change of teeth, the sleeping spirit around the head causes children to be imitative beings: They are one with their environment. Also the dreaming soul allows children to love their surroundings, especially the parents.

With the second dentition, this phase of development (the final forming of the head) is completed.[26] At the same time, something else happens with the chest.

In the chest, the physical and soul are present from the start, and the spirit is dreaming around it. And in the limbs all three aspects are *awake* from the beginning, only they are *unformed*. To summarize the situation at birth:

Head: formed body; developed but dreaming soul;
developed but sleeping spirit.

Limbs: awake body, soul and spirit, but all unformed.

The task of education is to develop the limb aspect and part of the chest aspect and let those awaken the dreaming spirit in the chest and the dreaming soul and sleeping spirit of the head.

If this were not the case, education would be impossible, since in order to educate the spirit we would have to be perfectly aware of all that the child could become. That would mean that the child could not be more intelligent, genial, or moral than the teacher. But since we only need to develop the will and feeling, the awakened child can then surpass the teacher just as it is possible for a servant to awaken his master. While being more intelligent than the children is not important for their development, the moral aspect is a little different. There, it is not just important that we strive to be as good as possible, but we need help from the world around us; without this help the children will probably not grow moral. We get this help from two sources.

As often mentioned already, the genius of language is one source of help. But when children are first born, they cannot yet make use of language any more than they can do gymnastics or art. In order to get their will to begin awakening the spirit, nature itself has to provide a substance that will begin the process of spirit waking. This substance is the mother's milk. It is formed in direct connection with the upper limbs and is the only substance we produce that carries the limb nature in it. The essence of the mother's will is present in the milk, and it serves to begin awakening the child's sleeping spirit.[27]

If we understood substances correctly, we would see that they have their own inner realities, and mother's milk has the inner need to awaken the sleeping spirit of the child. Substances are not the insignificant material entities that science imagines them to be. When we look at the world in this way, it becomes alive and imbued with meaning.

We can see that nature attends to the first phase of child development through the mother's milk, and we take up this task further through our use of language and deeds. The spirit of the head is already present at birth and has to be awakened. Our educational task is to awaken what is in the head, but we cannot add anything to it.

107

We need to be clear that the things we seem to teach the child (reading and writing, e.g.) are earthly conventions that are of no significance for the spiritual world. These conventions are only wholesome for the children when we bring them through the chest and limbs, i.e., artistically through drawing, painting and music. Because children had imitated the adult world before coming to us, it is possible to teach these conventions intellectually; but it is not healthy. Health-giving instruction proceeds from the limbs, through the arts, to awaken the intellect.

Aside from the things we teach them, children have other tasks as well. They have to grow, for instance. If the first phase of life, before the change of teeth, is principally about form, the grade school years are about life, i.e., growth and everything connected with it. Our teaching can, to some degree, influence this growth.

Everything connected with the formation of memory accelerates growth; in contrast, the cultivation of imagination retards growth.

At the beginning of each school year, and especially at the turning points of ages nine and twelve, the teacher should note how each child looks, and at the end of these years look at the children again. By emphasizing memory or imagination, the teacher can then balance out, to a degree, any tendencies towards lanky growth or stockiness.

We see again why it is so important for teachers to remain with their students. Only by following the same group for years can a teacher develop the right feeling for whether a child has too strong a tendency towards memory or towards imagination. This recognition is not to be developed via external measurements; it has to grow within the teacher's own imagination and memory. These concepts (memory and imagination) are not finished and defined separate realities, but interconnected flexible ones that have to comprehended as such.

The genius of nature raises the child after birth through the milk. During the grade school years, we continue this raising by feeding the children with art. Toward the end of grade school, the next phase, that of independent judgment, begins to sparkle in from the future. We will form the curriculum so as to invite this force from the future.

Endnotes

26 Change of teeth: Why does the change of teeth signal the conclusion of this phase of development? During the first seven years, the formative forces emanating from the head bring form to the organs below. The dense enamel of the baby teeth, however, is impervious to this process. As a result, instead of being reshaped

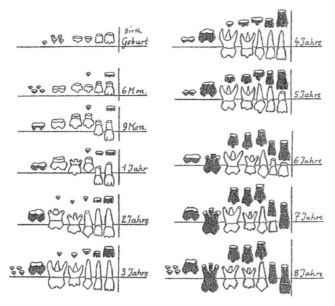

Average age at which teeth appear in children. White teeth are milk teeth; black teeth are permanent teeth. Jahr = Year (after Schad 1986)

like the other organs, a new creation must take place. The new teeth are larger and more defined than the milk teeth. Between the ages of six and seven, the crowns of the permanent teeth—the hardest substance in the human body—are complete (only the wisdom teeth remain unfinished at this point).

27 Mother's milk: The connection between the source of the mother's milk (the mammary glands) and the limbs can be seen in a seven-week embryo, when the mammary ridge (mammary line, milk line) appears as a band-like thickening of the epidermis, which extends on each side of the body from the base of the arm buds all the way to the leg buds below. Shortly thereafter, this "bridge" between the upper and lower limbs largely disappears, except for a region of the chest where 16–24 sprouts form that later canalize to the milk-conveying lactiferous ducts.

The composition of mother's milk is remarkably attuned to the nutritional needs of the growing infant and changes in accordance with them. The newborn does not yet have the forces to digest foreign substances and must be led gradually into that activity. Mother's milk allows this incarnation process to proceed

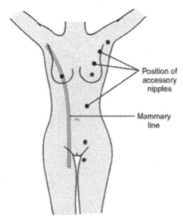

The mammary line (after Sadler 2000)

"gently." Extremely important at the outset is the protein-rich colostrum, which is rich in nutrients and contains high levels of antibodies that the infant needs before it has developed its own immune system.

Mother's milk has an extraordinarily low mineral content compared to the milk of animals and thus allows the "mineralization" of the body to proceed in a tempered and well-balanced way. On the other hand, the percentage of unsaturated long fatty acids, which relates to warmth internalization, is much higher in mother's milk than in animals.

Correspondent with the infant's changing biological needs, the protein content of the milk decreases as the lactose (milk sugar) content increases. The significance of this is explained by Otto Wolff as follows:

> Perhaps the most interesting fact about mother's milk is its high lactose content (7% as opposed to 4% for the cow's milk). It is a commonplace that milk sugar is found only in milk. One form of it, galactose, has a very specific task to perform. It has a clear affinity to the nerve-sense system, that is, to the upper organization and to its structuring formative forces that are especially active in the child. Galactose is also present in significant amounts in connective tissue (acid mucopolysaccharides, chondroitin sulfate), and from there guides structuring impulses into the supporting tissue. Milk sugar, the physiological sugar of the child, thus helps the ego organization stimulate and guide the impulses of growth and, as time goes on, to awaken consciousness. (Husemann & Wolff 2003, p. 102)

Resources: Husemann & Wolff (2003); Sadler (2000); Schmidt (1975)

Commentary: The body seen from soul and spirit: Sleeping, dreaming, waking

The form of the child's physical development has a relationship to how the child learns. Because the spirit in his head is asleep, he unconsciously feels he is part of all that is around him. Because his soul is dreaming, he abounds with love toward all around him, especially his parents. This statement is the background to why we do not want to intellectually wake up the child too soon. As long as he is asleep in his head, he imitates unconsciously. Intellectual education breaks this connection, and it is harder for the child to imitate because he is thinking about what he does instead of doing it.

Through this unconscious activity the child learns the mother tongue. As the child wakes up in thinking, he becomes conscious of the form and structure of language in grammar studies.

Study Questions

1. How do body, soul and spirit live within a child at birth?
2. Explain the quote: "We can awaken what is in the child, but we cannot implant a content into him."
3. How can we as teachers be "good comrades" of Nature?
4. How would you explain this concept to parents in relation to child development?
5. Give examples of curriculum content that is more earthly or conventional and content that is more cosmic or universal.
6. Why is an artistic approach to learning healthy for young children?

Lecture 12
September 3, 1919

Consideration of the human physical body must include its relationship with the surrounding natural world; only we must penetrate beyond superficial observation of nature into the deeper essence of its three kingdoms.

In the human being we perceive first the skeletal frame and muscles, then the circulatory system and the digestion with their respective organs, and finally the brain and nervous system. We have to connect these three with the natural environment.

We can begin with the head and the brain/nervous system, which is, as we have said, the oldest and most complete of the bodily structures. It has evolved through and then beyond the animal forms.

The task of the head during the first seven years is formative: Forces emanating from the head form the chest and limb systems with their organs below.[28] After the change of teeth, the head preserves the form and fills it with soul and spirit.

But there is a secret aspect to this formative process: At different times the head would like to turn the human being into the various shapes of the animal kingdom (wolf, lamb, etc.), but the torso and limbs dissolve these animal forms before the forms can move from their supersensible thought existence into physical manifestation.[29]

When the head tends too strongly toward animal formations and is stopped by the lower members, it has to revert to migraines and similar conditions in order to dissolve the forms.

The torso also has a relationship with the environment, only it is to the plant world in breathing and to combustion in digestion.

The breathing process creates carbon dioxide by combining oxygen from the air with carbon from the digestion. If we did not expel this carbon dioxide but released the oxygen from it and kept the carbon, plant forms would grow inside us. This is how plants "behave": They absorb carbon dioxide and keep the carbon while expelling the oxygen. This oxygen makes it possible for humans and animals to breathe. The plants assimilate the carbon and form sugars and starch out of it; human breathing is the reverse of this process. In the human being the breathing process continuously has the tendency to create plant forms, but the head and limbs arrest it. They force a reversal of plant tendencies.[30]

When the head and limbs are not able to arrest the plant-forming tendencies, we become ill. Human illnesses that arise in the torso are plant processes that the body could not expel, and we can look at the plant kingdom, especially the fruiting processes, as pictures of human illness. Of course, in its proper place outside of us, we are justified in enjoying the plant world; but unarrested within us it becomes illness. Medicine will become a science when it can bring illnesses into correspondence with specific plants.[31] Plant poisons, too, have a connection with health and illness; only it is more through the digestion.

Digestion appears to be a process of combustion in which we join oxygen from the breathing process with the substances we take in from the world as food. In reality, this combustion (oxidation) process is missing the beginning and the end of what combustion is outside the body. The first part of the process would be destructive to us, as we can see when we eat unripe fruit; we cannot begin the ripening process inside us. Similarly, we cannot eat overripe fruit and must excrete the digested substances before they reach that stage of disintegration. Our digestion is only the middle of the combustion process.

In the torso we see two processes interacting: the anti-plant breathing and the middle of the external process of combustion. When these two interact, there is the connection of the soul (the anti-plant process) and the body. When breathing joins with digestion (middle portion of an external process), there is the meeting of body and soul! The physical process begins and ends outside the body and is ensouled by breathing in between.

Medicine and healthcare will need to understand these things; researchers look for the bacterial causes of illnesses, but don't see that it is the inner, minute presence of vegetative processes that could not be expelled that has given the bacteria a hospitable environment in the first place. When we properly expel the plant processes, the bacteria do not find a suitable habitation within us.[32]

Now we have to look at the relationship of the skeleton and limbs to human vital processes.

Externally it appears that the movements of the limbs are purely mechanical. The bending of the arm, or walking, seem to be an exertion of forces similar to mechanical apparati. But if we could somehow photograph only the forces active in movement (without the person who is moving), we would see only shadows. The "I" does not live in the muscles and flesh, but rather in the forces that move the body. We find the "I" in the force that develops between our environment and us, e.g., between our feet and the earth. Our "I" lives in this force-body and drags the visible body around with it.

This body undertakes an unusual task. Its task is to dissolve the minerals that we ingest in our food, in order to prevent them from taking on their crystal forms within us. The head and torso cannot do much with the mineral content of our food, and it is the task of the limbs to dissolve those. Our limbs have the ongoing tendency to work against the mineral-building processes of the earth.

If the crystal-dissolving process of the limbs is too weak, then more severe illnesses such as gout and diabetes arise.[33] These are mineralization illnesses, and treating them requires making use of the decomposing matter that is created in the sense organs, in the brain and nervous system.

We can only understand the human body if we understand that it has to dissolve minerals, invert the plant nature, and rise above, overcome, the animal nature. Teachers should understand these processes, and we will see how we can build on them pedagogically.

Endnotes

28   Formative head forces: At birth the head typically makes up ¼ of the human body, by age seven only about 1/6, and in adulthood closer to 1/8.

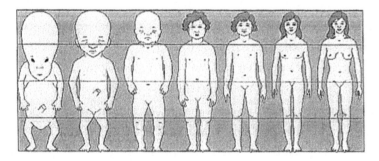

We see in the head—relative to other areas of the body—a very strong form tendency. This is evident in ossification of the skull bone sutures, in the extreme structural formation of the brain (during pregnancy, in the fetus approximately 250,000 new brain cells form every minute in order to reach the normal complement of 100 billion neurons at birth), as well as the complex structural and neurological differentiation of the eye and inner ear.

In the chest region we find organs that are reshaped by formative forces during the first seven years of life. The rib cage and lungs, for example, show this clearly.

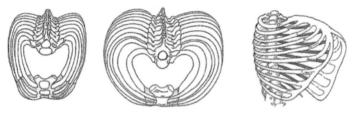

Ribcage from above of a newborn and an adult. Side view of a newborn's ribcage (from Kranich, et al. 1985)

29 The Head Wants to Create Animals: This rather surprising statement makes more sense when viewed in the context of Lecture 4, in which Rudolf Steiner speaks of how the wisdom with which the beaver builds its lodge comes not through a long and complicated schooling in architecture, as it would need to in the case of humans, but is possible because the beaver's physical body is formed in just such a way that it is the perfect instrument for building lodges and dams. Who, then, is the beaver's teacher? Its own physical body and the instincts that go with it.

Whence arises the one-sided/specialized wisdom of the animal's physical body and the corresponding instinctual capacities? In a lecture, "The Human Soul and the Animal Soul" (Berlin, Nov. 10, 1910), Rudolf Steiner explores this topic more extensively. Here just a small sample:

What do we really mean when we speak of "spirit"?
We ascribe to spirit that reality which we ourselves

experience, as it were, in our intelligence. Through
our intelligence we execute one thing or another; we
bring the forces of different beings into an ensemble.
This creative intelligence of ours has a particular
characteristic. In that it enters into us in temporal
existence and is a creative force, we form a concept of
intelligence, of reason, of creative intelligence, and then
we look at the universe around us.—We should have to
be very shortsighted before we could possibly ascribe
intelligence, all that we call "spirit," to ourselves
alone.... What lives within us as intelligence is also
outspread in space and time, is actively at work in
space and time....

    If we look at any particular animal, we see before
us a self-enclosed existence, creative in the same way as
the spirit outspread in space and time is creative. And
a feeling will dawn in us of why those who knew what
they were doing called this spirit working actively in
the animal, the "astral body.".... They said: "The spirit
lives in the ordering of the universe and in a single
animal organism we see a certain conclusion, we see
the spirit confined within the space bounded by the
animal's skin."

When (a thoughtful individual) sees the wasp building its
nest, he says to himself: There I can see intelligence springing
forth as it were, from the animal organization itself.... Think of
the forces of intelligence which man was obliged to apply and
master in his own soul life before he was able to produce paper.
But the wasps have been able to do it for thousands of years! For
what is to be found in the wasps' nest is exactly the same as what
man produces as "paper."

    So we see unmistakably that what flows out of man's intelli-
gence springs from the animal organism with full vigor of life.

In short, what lives as intelligence in the astral body of a human being (and which permeates all the way to the etheric body and is mirrored in the physical body) goes a step further in animals. It incarnates completely into the physical body of the animal. This one-sided form of the astral body is filled with cosmic wisdom, the wisdom that now appears in the animal's anatomy and physiology, in its instincts, and in the perfect way it fits into its natural environment (ecological niche). In each animal the astral body is fully incarnated, and the physical body is visible expression of that particular astral body. This embodied wisdom of the animal world is something we access at a different level. We access it through our unspecialized thinking capacity that allows us to understand the myriad animals and their corresponding behaviors that we find in the world around us.

In the context of Lecture 12, this points to forces working from the human head down into the rest of the organism—astral forces—that in nature have produced the animal world. These forces, if not balanced out by that which lives in our torso and limbs, would carry out their time-honored task of incarnating astral intelligence all the way into the physical—in the form of animals. In this sense, the head forces that we so badly need would, if left on their own, go too far in their formative tendencies and bind the fluidity of human thinking into fixed, one-sided thought forms.

Resources: Poppelbaum (2014); Steiner (1910)

30 Humans-Plants: If the bronchial tree seen below is turned upside down then it appears very much like a tree, one that branches some twenty times, thereby building around a million terminal branches. From these, in turn, "hang" 300 million grape-like alveoli (whose total surface is about 120 square meters).

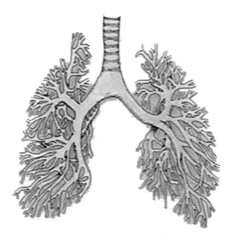

Human bronchial tree (from: www.medean.luc.edu)

Not only is this tree upside down, but it is also inside out! It is hollow on the inside, and around it is a world of solid substance—the human body. This upside-down hollow tree does not build up new substance through its activity, it consumes bodily substance. Through our breathing activity the human body is consumed. If it were not balanced by the intake of food through the digestive system, it would consume us completely. (As many of us know from experience: The less you breathe—i.e., the less exercise you get—the more weight you gain!)

Our bronchial tree gives off oxygen in its periphery through the alveoli. This is the critical element in "aerobic respiration," for it makes possible the oxidation of our ingested food into carbon dioxide and water, with a corresponding release of energy. The carbon dioxide that is freed we take back into the lungs at the periphery of tree. In other words, at the outer periphery of our bronchial tree (the alveoli) we have a "gas exchange" where oxygen is given off into the body's bloodstream and, conversely, carbon dioxide is taken from that bloodstream and given off into the lungs and then the outer world.

A normal tree also gives off oxygen and takes in carbon dioxide in its periphery (through the leaves). That tree, however, builds its organism out of this carbon dioxide (combined with water and light energy). We do not, we breathe out the carbon dioxide through the base of our tree (throat and mouth). Imagine, as Rudolf Steiner suggests hypothetically, if we were to hold onto the carbon and only the oxygen from the carbon dioxide were expelled? An average person, for example exhales around 400 liters carbon dioxide every 24 hours. If that person lived 71 years, s/he would exhale approximately 20.4 tons of carbon dioxide during one lifetime, which would contain 5.6 tons of carbon if the oxygen were removed (Leber, 2002, pp. 384–385)!

If we kept all this carbon within, it would have to be assimilated within our organism, where it would combine chemically with other substances, creating organic compounds of various kinds. Impossible? Plants do it all the time—maybe we could too! But, alas, we don't get to find out because our head and limb systems say "no" to it and work constantly against this possibility. The catabolic processes we find coming from the nervous system of the head, and the dynamic movement-impulses from the limbs, break down substances, whereby energy is released and plant substance devoured. Instead of a plant kingdom, we find just one tree, an upside-down one that is hollow on the inside and that consumes the organic substance around it (the body) rather than building it up within.

Resources: Constanza (2013); Leber (2002)

31 Plants and Illness: Generally speaking, a healthy organism has an internal equilibrium between its members, whereas a sick organism has lost that balance. When such disharmony arises, certain members develop excessively, while others atrophy. In the threefold understanding of the human being, the polarity of the upper nerve-sense system and the lower metabolic-limb system is balanced by the rhythmical system. If the upper organization grows too dominant, it results in stagnation of metabolic activity, excessive breakdown and hardening (sclerosis). If the lower organization becomes too vigorous, this manifests in inflammatory reactions with accompanying warmth, redness and swelling.

Looking to the plant, it has long been observed that a similar polarity exists there, too—in this case between the contracted, hardening and mineralizing tendencies of the root and the rarified, expansive, warmth-related characteristics of the flowering pole of the plant. Mediating between these is the rhythmical leaf activity of the plant middle. Relating these to similar qualities in the human threefoldness—root to head, blossom to metabolic-limb system, and leafing to the rhythmical system—we come again, as in the bronchial tree, to an upside-down human being.

In the world of plants, however, the emphasis of one pole over the other does not lead to illness; it provides, rather, a creative principle for producing an endless diversity of plant forms. Some plants develop enormous blossoms, with little leaf

Rafflesia (from lazerhorse.org)

or root development—for example, the official state flower of Indonesia, the "giant flower" (*Rafflesia*) that develops no stem, leaves or true roots, but has flowers that can reach over three feet in diameter and weigh 22 lbs. Other plants can be predominantly stem (such as *Equisetum*), leaf (such as ferns), or hypertrophy into huge fruits (such as pumpkins and melons), etc. And it is just such one-sided developments of the archetypal plant (Goethe) that can turn "normal plants" into medicinal ones.

A brief look at the mint family (the labiatae), which includes rosemary, sage, thyme, lavender, and many more well-known herbs, can provide a hint of how one-sided qualities in a plant can influence the human organism when prepared and applied in the appropriate manner. The labiates, with their square stems and wrinkled leaves often appear dried out. This comes from the strong permeation of the entire plant—not just the blossom—with warmth processes. The leaves thus become carriers of the volatile oils that give these plants their characteristic odor. Like all plants, labiates need the sun's warmth to develop, but they take it up to such a degree that they become warmth bearers themselves.

Labiates are thus able, in their therapeutic application, to support the warmth processes of the human organism. The nuanced differences between the various members of this family lead to therapeutic applications that assist our warmth organization in ailments ranging from pulmonary maladies (tuberculosis, for example) and menstrual disturbances, to states of exhaustion following fever, influenza and liver ailments, to name just a few uses. The strong, inner-warming and stimulating effects of a rosemary bath after a long day on the front lines is well known to many experienced Waldorf teachers, of course!

(This small nibble regarding the therapeutic potential found in the unbelievable diversity of the plant kingdom might lead the interested reader to explore this theme in Wilhelm Pelikan's outstanding resource, *Healing Plants*, published in two volumes by Mercury Press, 1997.)

32 Bacteria: In a land where antibacterial soap has become the norm (despite clear findings about its negative effects), it is evident that bacteria (microbes) are still seen by many (most) as the primary cause of countless illnesses. This concern is accompanied, of course, by the heavy use of antibiotics.

From the perspective of holistic medicine, such a simple cause-effect explanation (bacteria being the cause, illness the effect) does not get to the bottom of the issue. One illustrative analogy (Husemann & Wolff 2003) is that of an explosion. The real cause of an explosion is not the spark that sets it off, but rather the potential energy contained in the explosive itself. From a holistic perspective, the invasion by bacteria, like the spark, can be seen as merely a symptom for a pre-existing condition that was just waiting to manifest. The spark would not catch— the bacteria would not spread—if the necessary conditions for it (the explosives) were not already present. So viewed, infectious diseases could be termed "information diseases" because they inform us of a pre-existing disorder or deficiency. So seen, bacterial infection is not a primary cause, but actually an indicator of more deep-seated issues.

By contrast, the growing interest in probiotics (yogurt and kefir, e.g.) shows an awareness of the significance of healthy microbes in the life of an organism and in disease prevention. For example, the trillions of bacteria that line the gut and the surface of the skin form colonies known as the "microbiome" that are essential for a healthy human organism, for example. This is no small matter—the weight of the microbiome is roughly equal to that of the brain. Understanding how this dynamic, constantly changing world of microbes is integrated into the life of organisms—both in health and illness—presents an exciting field of exploration for modern medicine.

Resources: Chopra, & Tanzi (2015); Husemann & Wolff (2003)

33 Gout/Diabetes

GOUT. Gout is a disease that produces an excess of uric acid in the blood stream. As the final breakdown-product of a form of protein (purines), uric acid then converts to sodium urate crystals that precipitate from the blood and deposit in joints and other tissues. Related to this, Rudolf Steiner and Ita Wegman (1925) discuss in *Fundamentals of Therapy* how, if the ego organization (which Steiner speaks of in this lecture as active in the forces that move our limbs) is too weak to control the breakdown (metabolism) of uric acid, then instead of being excreted "outward" in the urine, it is excreted "inward," where it deposits in the joints.

DIABETES. Whereas gout is involved in the breakdown and excretion of protein crystals, with diabetes it is carbohydrate crystallization that is the issue. For diabetics, the breakdown of carbohydrates into glucose (blood sugar) during digestion is not the problem. This catabolic process—says Rudolf Steiner—is brought about primarily by the astral body. A further, necessary step, however, involves the permeation of the carbohydrates by the ego organization. In individuals suffering from diabetes, this process does not take place sufficiently, as Steiner and Wegman point out:

In diabetes mellitus the case is as follows: The ego-organization, as it submerges in the astral and etheric realm, is so weakened that it can no longer effectively accomplish its action upon the sugar substance (1925).

As a result, certain necessary stages of healthy glucose catabolism are missing. Normally the ego organization works through the production of insulin in the pancreas to permeate the sugar and make it capable of being stored as glycogen in the liver. Without this, any consumption of sugar is for the organism like being flooded with a foreign substance. So, despite large amounts of glucose flowing in the blood, the diabetic cannot utilize it and suffers from sugar deficiency.

The key role that the limb system plays in the activation of the ego organization is also revealed by the fact that in earlier times the only known way to treat diabetes was through heavy physical work to the point of exhaustion. Such intensified use of the limbs helps incarnate the ego to a degree that it is able to permeate the sugar with its own organizing activity.

Resources: Husemann & Wolff (2003); Steiner & Wegman (1925)

Commentary: Physical body: microcosm, macrocosm

One of the most interesting part of this lecture is to grasp that during the first seven years, intense forces from the head work to shape the rest of the physical form. The head is constantly trying to make the human body into animal forms. This processes stops around age 7, and the forces move into soul activity, into thoughts and images.

We can ask ourselves how different a bear-like influence would be from a fox-influence? Another way would be to ask ourselves if the child's movements and soul qualities have more of the lethargic quality of the bear or a more sly quality of a fox. This is an imaginative exercise, and we have to be careful not to judge the child based on this. We have to continually observe and be able to change what comes to us.

Study Questions

1. Relate the idea that the human head tends to create animal forms to:
    a. the second grade curriculum, and
    b. the fourth grade curriculum.
2. How is the human being related to the plant world?
3. Compare various plant families to stages of the growth of a child.
4. Compare the process of combustion in a plant and in the human being. Where in the curriculum can you deal with this?
5. Give three examples of mechanical processes performed by the human skeleton. Describe the forces at work in each.
6. Where in the curriculum do we find support/opportunities for the actual processes of:
    a. dissolving the mineral in the human being;
    b. reversing the plant world in the human being; and
    c. spiritualizing the animal world in the human being?

Lecture 13
September 4, 1919

We can use what we have learned in these lectures to understand children's behavior when we keep in mind the twofold polarity of the limbs and the head.

Recall the difficult idea that the limbs are the head turned inside out. The head is formed, in a sense, from internal pressure; it is "inflated;" the limbs are "compressed" from without inwards.

The same spirit-soul forces stream through your hands (from above) and your feet (from below) as course through your body into your head. The stream of spirit-soul is obstructed by the human being as a river is when it's dammed, and the effect of this streaming is that the spirit-soul absorbs the human body. That is why we shed and peel on the outside. Internally the chest and abdomen build up the body in opposition to the destructive spirit-soul.

We see from this that the limbs are the most spiritual part of the body. They consume matter rather than create it. When they are not active enough, the torso creates an overabundance of matter: It creates fat. Fat creates a blockage for the spirit-soul, obstructing its path to the head.[34] Children should really not be allowed to grow fat under normal circumstances; appropriate nourishment should allow them to avoid becoming too fat. Doing otherwise is an interference with cosmic evolution, since it prevents the spirit-soul from entering the child.

When the spirit-soul is able to flow in the body, it enters the head and splashes matter back like water meeting a weir.[35] This pounding of matter against matter causes a subtle disintegration process and that is how the nerves are formed; the nerve pathways are pathways of decayed matter. The spirit needs this dead matter, since it can only fill human beings where the matter in their body is dead.

The spirit-soul approaches the body from without, absorbing and consuming the living substance in order to move within on paths of dead matter. Living matter absorbs the spirit and does not let it through. Only dead matter is spiritually permeable. Thus blood absorbs the spirit, but the nerves for the spirit are like transparent glass is to light. They let the spirit through.

The difference between the living substance that is opaque to the spirit and the dead matter that is transparent is very important. When people work with their limbs, they swim in spirit. This is the spirit without, and not the spirit coursing through the human being. Whenever we use our limbs we splash around in spirit; the spirit is excessively active. By contrast, when we do mental work we are dealing with the spirit within; it is the body that is then excessively active.

~ Limb activity: Cosmic spirit is active; human spirit does only a little by guiding the work.

~ Mental activity: Human spirit is active through inner excitement of matter.

These things are very important for understanding human work, whether physical or mental. Too much physical work means that we are surrounding by the spirit too much, leading to a need for excessive amounts of sleep. This, in turn, causes the blood to overheat, so that our activity cannot be transformed properly.

Lethargy is a different problem. Lethargic people fidget and move their limbs about aimlessly. They get tired because their aimless movements tire them out, whereas industrious people draw the spirit into themselves consciously, through purposeful work, and therefore need less sleep.

Thus purposeful activity is what we have to strive for with children. This means acting according to the demands of the world around us, and not just acting as the body demands.

Calisthenics is an example of a purely physical activity; it must be balanced with purposeful movement such as eurythmy. By balancing the child's physical education with eurythmy, we foster a healthy harmony between the need for sleep and wakefulness.

That exercise has been made into sport is a result of materialism. Sport in excess is practical Darwinism; it drags human activity into the animal domain from which Darwinism supposes we emerged.[36]

These are strong words, but we must understand the social effect of what we ask of the children.

With mental work, we always see an accompanying decomposition of matter. Excessive mental work leaves us with too much dead matter and disturbs our sleep, just like excessive physical work leaves us drowsy.

If we listen to people who actually say something new and mentally demanding, we become tired from the inner effort. Here, too, there are two aspects, just as in the difference between purposeful and aimless work. If we accompany our thinking with interest and warmth, that is, with real feeling, then this is a chest activity that mitigates the decomposing influence of mental work. But dry reading and memorization foster the dying of our own matter. Warm interest fosters blood activity and inhibits the disturbance of sleep.

We see how senseless final examinations are, when students cram great quantities of information that do not interest them, thereby disturbing sleep and affecting health. It would be best for education if final examinations were dropped altogether.

Teachers know how their students are doing at the end of the year and do not need those harmful examinations. We should work, quietly at first, toward having society think differently about these questions.

You must think about these things: Eurythmy is an activity filled with purpose, that it spiritualizes work,[37] and that interesting instruction brings blood and life to intellectual work.

We have to bring spirit to external work and our life's blood to mental work. The former is significant in teaching and social life, and the latter is significant in teaching and health.

Endnotes

34 Excess Fat Blocks the Spirit-soul in Children: The torso, that wants to become plant (see Lecture 12), also creates as surplus matter a plant substance: fat. In the plant, fats arise in the leaves, but wander at night primarily into the fruit and seed regions (the metabolic pole). This takes place most intensely in areas of the earth where there is great warmth (the tropics).

The relationship of unsaturated fats to warmth can be seen in their lack of form and malleable consistency. They also burn intensely and have a low melting point. Interestingly, these fats do not let warmth through, which makes them excellent warmth insulators—keeping seals and whales warm in the frigid arctic seas, for example.

Fats are not ensouled and can thus be removed surgically without pain. That same quality allows fatty tissues to serve not only as excellent padding when sat upon, but also in the soles of our feet and the palms of our hands.

One could thus say that fat is actually a manifestation of warmth in material form. Instead of producing warmth as a medium for ego activity in the limbs (and elsewhere), fat deposits

have not been called into activity and have become material—
this form of bodily substance is not permeated with soul forces
and does not let the ego activity mediating warmth through. Too
much of this substance in children, says Rudolf Steiner, blocks
the flow of the soul-spiritual forces to the head at a time when
that flow is critical for brain development.

Interestingly, the saturated fats, in contrast to the unsaturated
ones discussed above, play a central role in the head region,
where they are the main component of the myelin sheathes found
in the white matter of the brain. These "head-pole fats" are much
denser and more formed than the unsaturated fats of the torso
and have a higher melting point.

Resources: Husemann & Wolff (2003); Schmidt (1975)

35 Spirit/Soul Spraying Back Like Water Meeting a Weir.

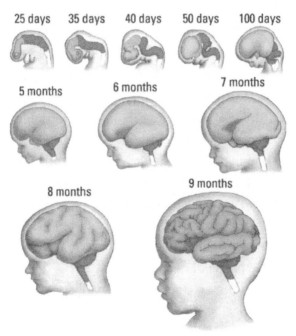

Human Brain Development (from Researchgate.net)

The image Rudolf Steiner brings of the soul-spiritual flowing through the body until it reaches the forehead, where it is dammed up and must flow back upon itself—thereby forming the dead pathways of the central nervous system—can easily be imagined in conjunction with the images above. As the neural tube develops, it appears to be blocked in its forward movement (ascensus) and begins to bend and then kink back on itself (40 days). At the same time, the spherical vesicle seen at the front of the tube—the telencephalon—begins to turn in a semispiral (40–50 days). From there it increases rapidly in size (50 days and on), while at the same time flowing back over and enveloping the other sections of the brain. The wall of the telencephalon thickens in the process and eventually develops ridges (gyri) and furrows (sulci) as a result of cell migration. The telencephalon becomes the cerebrum, the largest and most highly developed part of the brain. It is composed of the two cerebral hemispheres that are connected by the corpus callosum. At the back of the cerebrum we can see the cerebellum and medulla oblongata peeking out.

Resources: Rohen (2001)

36 Sport in Excess: This statement may cause antipathy and rejection in many sport lovers, but it is important to note at the outset that Rudolf Steiner is referring here to "sport in excess." An example of this tendency was manifest to me (MH) when I attended my 30th high school reunion. During a tour of the gym and weight room, I learned that students were no longer allowed to play three sports during a school year as they had in my day (football in the fall, basketball or wrestling in the winter...), but had to choose one sport and focus on it all year long. In the off-season that means more time in the weight room building up the specific set of muscles needed for the specific position one plays in the specific sport one has chosen, and practice, practice, practice to fine tune the specialized movements needed for that position.

As was discussed in Endnote 16, animals differ from humans in that their astral bodies are fully incarnated into the physical body, thereby shaping it in a one-sided and specialized direction, accompanied by the corresponding behavior (instincts). In the intensive training practiced in many sports today, we see how tremendous time and effort is invested in specific body and movement-shaping practices, thereby drawing the athlete's astral body (soul forces) into the body in a very one-sided way. The astral forces are absorbed more and more in the service of specific requirements of the body that fit into a certain niche within the sport they are dedicating so much effort to. They are working in a direction that is realized to perfection in the animal kingdom. If the athlete has talent, this narrow focus often absorbs a high proportion of their waking life.

All of this is infused with extreme competitiveness, a kind of Darwinian "survival of the fittest" mindset. The "winner takes all" mentality is pounded into anyone who hopes to succeed in their sport. If you can't beat out your competition, then "natural selection" will remove you to the bench.

To what end? This isn't about play, it is about winning, about surviving through endless competition to put yourself on top, because you have become the "fittest"—the fittest in your narrow niche of bodily brilliance!

So how is this different from practicing a musical instrument, for example? In the latter—which can also be time-intensive if one wants to "get really good"—the capacities developed are a means to "revealing" the music. This activity is not one that "drives" the soul into the body, but allows the soul to weave with the music in such a way that the music can be revealed for that moment. This kind of activity also engages a much larger range of senses than most sports.

Of course, sport represents for many in the modern world something very different from what was just described. It provides a regenerative opportunity to balance out the one-sided, stress-filled, head-dominated activities of "normal life." It provides an "out-breath" thereto. This is not what Rudolf Steiner is referring to when he says "sport in excess." By contrast, "playing" sports as recreation, as an integrative team experience, or as a means for learning to penetrate one's body more harmoniously, can be seen as a harmonizing element on the way to a healthy body and a lively inner life.

As this endnote had just been completed, a new issue of *Time Magazine* (September 4, 2017) appeared with the picture of a ten year old boy playing baseball on the cover, accompanied by the heading: *How Kid Sports Turned Pro (Crazy Travel, Crazy Costs, Crazy Stress)*. Inside the magazine, the article is billed as: "The Kid's Sports Machine—How Your Child's Rec League Turned into a $15 Billion Industry!" The article goes on to describe how relentless training is essential for top players. How the new reality for America's aspiring young athletes at all skill levels, and in virtually every sport, is to be "swept up by a youth-sport economy that increasingly resembles the pros at increasingly early ages." Moreover, "a growing body of research shows that intense early specialization in a single sport increases the risk of injury, burnout and depression." This, and much more described in the article, is what Rudolf Steiner would call "sport in excess."

Resource: Gregory (2017)

37 Eurythmy: Isn't eurythmy similar to sport? As a profession it too requires years of training and practice. One key difference, as Rudolf Steiner says in this lecture, is that eurythmy is "from meaning-permeated outer activity." Although this may not seem obvious to everyone—as many Waldorf high school students will exclaim!—eurythmy was developed as an art of movement that expresses that which lives in speech. The emphasis is not on the overt content, but on that which lives in the dynamic of the speech—in the tone, in the way the words are formed, in the rhythm and tempo, in its gravity or whimsicality, and in the force and expression that lives in the sequence of the vowels and consonants. The eurythmist lives into the way that all these elements are formed into words, verses and sentences as they live in the human soul—and makes this visible! In the sense that Paul Klee speaks of art, that it does not reproduce the visible, but makes visible, eurythmy does not just turn speech into outer movement, it makes visible something that lives in the human soul as it expresses itself through speech. In a similar sense, eurythmy also engages the elements of music in movement to "make visible" something that lives therein. Because eurythmy is not just bodily movement, but "meaning-filled" in that it brings the inner to outer expression, it has a very different effect on the human being than excessive sport.

Resource: Van der Pals (1984)

Commentary: Relationship of the child to the world

Steiner expresses concern about children who are too fat. He speaks about the importance of nutrition and movement. He also recommends movement for the teacher because in moving our limbs we are involved in spiritual activity, and when we do spiritual work matter is active in us. An example is shown that when we cram to prepare our lessons or for a test, we become exhausted. To counter this we get up and move around to feel refreshed again. If there is meaning in our movements when we work, we draw spirit into us. When we work consciously with our hands or body, we are refreshed. We need to be active with a purpose.

We also need to guide the children into making meaningful movement. Steiner points out the benefit of eurythmy for healthy child development. The more we can alternate gymnastics with eurythmy, the more harmony we bring to the sleeping and waking life, as well as strengthening the child's will.

Study Questions

1. Read aloud this verse by Rudolf Steiner, given for eurythmy (11 July 1924):

   I seek within
   The working of creative forces,
   The life of creative powers.
   Earth's gravity is telling me
   Through the word of my feet,
   Air's wafting forms are telling me
   Through the singing of my hands,
   Heaven's light is telling me
   Through the thinking of my head,
   How the great world in man
   Speaks, sings, thinks.

   Now describe how the forces of the spirit flow into and out of the human being.

2. Describe two human beings, an ascetic and a bon vivant, in terms of how the spirit works within their physical bodies.

3. Why does Mephistopheles have Faust sign his name to the pact in blood?

4. Why does it matter if physical movement is done with a purpose? What different kinds of purposes are there? Give examples. Compare eurythmy and sport.

5. What does Steiner mean by "practical Darwinism"?

6. How can you deepen the interest of the children in your lessons?

7. Are tests and exams necessary in Waldorf schools?

Lecture 14
September 5, 1919

Our considerations of the human body have clearly revealed a distinct threefold picture: the head, the torso and the limbs. The limbs are more complicated than people realize, because they are inserted into us and in reality represent an extension of forces streaming in from the periphery.

In the head we have the entire human being: The nose is a stunted torso, and the jaws are stunted limbs. The nose is to some extent a metamorphosed lung, and the mouth with its jaws is plainly connected with digestion, metabolism and nutrition. It extends the limb nature into the head, albeit in stunted form.[38]

By contrast, the limbs can be seen as a transformation of the upper and lower jaws. Seen in reality, the spiritual head is enclosed in the periphery, and the shoulders and hips (the points where the limbs insert into the torso) are like the teeth. The limbs in their movement "consume" the body! At death, the spiritual head has completely consumed the physical body. But even during life, our organism continually slips into the wide-open mouth of our spirituality. The devotion required of us expresses itself in the form of our body. The head and the limbs form the two opposite extremes, and the torso creates the balance between them.

The torso also includes the other two principles within it. Toward the top, the torso tends to become head-like, while toward the bottom it assumes a more stretched-out limb nature. Near the top, the actual head stops the chest from becoming head, and the closest the chest gets is the formation of the larynx, which is a stunted head (in German, *Kehlkopf*, literally "throat-

139

head").[39] In the sounds of speech we find attempts by the larynx to become a head, only those are thwarted by the head itself. In nasal sounds, the nose thwarts the larynx's attempt at becoming a nose. So human speech is the result of the head constricting wavelike attempts of the larynx to create parts of the head in the air.

We can thus see how when the head development is completed (around seven years old) we can give speech a kind of soul skeleton through grammar, and this replaces the learning of language by imitation. By teaching writing and reading out of [correct] speech, we do something similar to the formation of the second teeth.

In the other direction, downwards, the torso tends toward limb nature. When the insertion of the limbs continues into the torso, it coarsens into the formation of the sexual organs.[40]

Just as in the early years of grade school we insert what entered through the teeth into the soul, so in the last years of grade school we must bring to the child's soul what enters through the limbs and finds expression in puberty.

As the soul teeth (the capacity to learn) appear at seven, so imagination and inner warmth, the capacity to fill things with inner love, appears between twelve and fifteen. During the later elementary years, we must stimulate the imagination continually in everything the students have to learn. In physiology we can do that by comparing the sense organs with technological innovations (the eye with a camera lens, e.g.). In geometry and arithmetic, too, we must appeal to the imagination by asking the students to visualize surfaces and situations inwardly.

As teachers we must keep our instruction alive so it stimulates the imagination. We can only do that by imbuing the material with feeling-will. In the upper grades this will have the strange effect of building a harmonious community of teachers and students. An approach that isn't fresh, isn't new, even if it repeats what we once created ourselves, becomes frozen, petrified.

This leads us to what the teachers themselves must be. They must never grow bitter or pedantic. They must keep their imagination alive. For bitterness or pedantry in the teacher is not just wrong, it is immoral.

Pedagogical enthusiasm will not grow without contemplation of the threefold human being and how each part contains stunted versions of the other two. If this thought becomes inwardly alive, it will fill you with the strength to imbue your pedagogical morality with enthusiasm.

Materialistic ideas lead what forms human intellectuality to become slow and lazy, but when we receive ideas from the spirit laziness must flee. These ideas, however, can only enter indirectly through imagination.

In the second half of the 19th century, people began fearing that accepting the imagination would tempt the soul toward accepting untruth. We must be able to accept imagination while remaining steadfast and courageous in pursuing the truth.

A need for imagination, courage for the truth, and a feeling of responsibility: Those three should be the motto of the teacher.

> Enliven Imagination
> Stand for the Truth.
> Feel Responsibility.

Endnotes

38   The Nose as Stunted Lung in the Head: As we saw already in Lecture 10, the jaws represent the limb pole of the head. The nose, on the other hand—as Steiner points out in this lecture—can be viewed as a metamorphosed lung. This becomes more

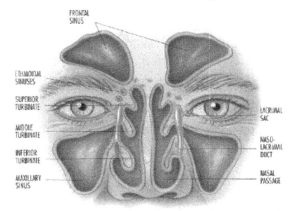

Nasal Cavity with Turbinates (from www.aaaai.org)

obvious when one looks into the nasal cavity and discovers that in the enfolded spaces created by the protruding turbinate tissue ridges one sees the "stunted" beginning of what, with further invagination and branching into passageways and alveoli, could becomes something like the lungs. These spaces and the turbinate ridges also begin preparing the air for the lungs by warming and moisturizing it as it passes through.

39   Torso–the Head Tendency: As the rib cage makes evident, the torso has the tendency to become spherical at the top (caudal pole) and to open more and more as it descends, culminating in the radial floating ribs, which are not connected in the front. The mobility of the ribs increases, too, as we move further from the head. The contractive tendency seen here at the top of the ribcage reaches its culmination in the uppermost region of the torso, where we find the larynx.

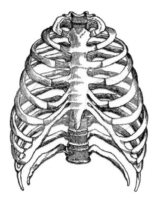
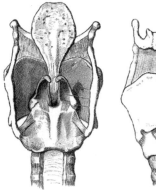
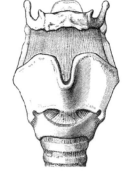

Human Rib Cage
(from www.pinterest.com)

The Human Larynx, front and back
(from www.daviddarling.info)

With its head-like qualities, the larynx has received the name *Kehlkopf* (throat-head) in the German language. The larynx does not, however, manage to achieve "headness" all the way, as Rudolf Steiner points out. It is composed of nine pieces of cartilage, which do not reach the density of the ossified head bones. Normally, when organs form, the cartilage stage is just an intermediate embryonic one, which moves rapidly to a more defined form that then ossifies. The larynx, however, remains in this premature cartilage stage, as if it were not able to complete its development. The larynx also remains open at the back and does not achieve the complete closure of a sphere.

The larynx reveals its head-like tendency in yet another way, however, as the form giver to the flow of air that passes through it. The formation of the human voice has three components. On the one hand we have something like a wind instrument in the air flow (respiration) upward from the from diaphragm and chest region, followed by a string instrument through the vibration of the vocal cords embedded in the larynx and regulated through the oscillation of the two arytenoid cartilages. Lastly, the head itself becomes involved in the articulation of the air streaming up from the larynx. In all, nineteen points between the vocal cords and the lips are involved in the shaping of that airflow (among others, the lips, teeth, plates, tongue, nasal cavity and uvula). As Rudolf Steiner observes, this shaping of the air stream is itself an attempt to become head, which is the form pole of the human organism.

Resources: Tortora & Derrickson (2013); Rohen (2007); Kranich 1980

40 Resources Consulted

Amundson, R. (2007). *The Changing Role of the Embryo in Evolutionary Thought—Roots of Evo-Devo*. New York: Cambridge University Press.

Barfield, O. (1988). *Saving the Appearances*. Middletown, CT: Wesleyan University Press.

Bauer, F. & Holdrege, M. (1985). Ist der Mensch Sklave seiner Gene? In *Das Wagnis Erziehung*. H. Ganser, Ed. Wien, Köln: Boehlau.

Benninghoff-Goerttler. (1977). *Lehrbuch der Anatomie des Menschen*. Bd. 3. Muenchen-Berlin: Urban und Schnausenberger.

Blechschmidt, E. (2004). *The Ontogenetic Basis of Human Anatomy*. Berkeley, CA: N. Atlantic Books.

Carroll, S. (2005). *Endless Forms Most Beautiful—The New Science of Evo-Devo*. New York: Norton.

Chopra, D. & Tanzi, R. (2015). *Super Genes*. New York: Harmony Books.

Chung, K. & Chung, H. (2012). *Gross Anatomy*. Baltimore: Lippincott, Williams & Wilkins.

Constanzo, L. (2013). *Physiology*. Philadelphia: Saunders.

Davy, J. (1985). The Evolution of Evolution. In *Hope, Evolution and Change*. UK: Hawthorne Press.

Dietz, K. (1990). *Metamorphosen des Geistes*, Bd. III. Stuttgart: Fries Geistesleben.

Goethe, J. (1988). *Goethe: Scientific Studies*. D. Miller, editor. New York: Suhrkamp.

Gould, S. (2002). *The Structure of Evolutionary Theory*. Cambridge, MA: Belknap/Harvard Press.

_____. (1977). *Ontogeny and Phylogeny*. Cambridge, MA: Belknap/Harvard Press.

Gregory, S. "How Kid Sports Turned Pro." *Time Magazine* (September 4, 2017).

Grohmann, G. (1996). *The Plant*. Kimberton, PA: Biodynamic Association.

Hanson, N. (1958). *Patterns of Discovery*. Cambridge, UK: Cambridge Univ. Press.

Hesse, H. (1973). *Autobiographical Writings*. New York: Farrar, Strauss & Giroux.

Holdrege, C. (2005). *The Giraffe's Long Neck*. Nature Institute Perspectives #4.

Holdrege, M. (2009). Phenomenology: Husserl's Philosophy and Goethe's Approach to Science, in *From Beach to Savannah*. Ann Arbor: Proquest.

Husemann, A. (2013). *Human Hearing*. Great Barrington, MA: SteinerBooks.

Husemann, G. & Wolff, O. (2003). *The Anthroposophic Approach to Medicine*. Vol. III. Spring Valley, NY: Mercury Press.

Kipp, F. (2005). *Childhood and Human Evolution*. Hillsdale, NY: Adonis.

Julius, F. (2000). *Fundamentals of a Phenomenological Study of Chemistry*. Fair Oaks, CA: AWSNA Publications.

_____. (1969). *Metamorphose*. Stuttgart: JC Mellinger.

Kranich, E. (2003). *Der Innere Mensch und sein Leib*. Stuttgart: Freies Geistesben.

_____. (1999). *Thinking beyond Darwin*. Hudson, NY: Lindesfarne.

_____. (1980). Die Menschliche Wesenheit und die Sprache. Erziehungskunst, 7/8.

Kranich, Juenemann, et al. (1992). *Formenzeichnen*. Stuttgart: Freies Geistesleben.

Larsen, Matter & Gebo. (1998). *Human Origins. The Fossil Record*. Long Grove, IL: Waveland Press.

Leber, S. (2002). *Kommentare zur Rudolf Steiners Vortraege zur Allgemeine Menschenkunde*. Stuttgart: Freies Geistesleben.

Lehrs, E. (1958). *Man or Matter*. London: Faber & Faber.

Lindenberg, C. (1981). Geistbewusstsein im Abendland. In *Die Drei* 12/81.

Losos, Mason, et al. (2016). *Biology*. Boston: McGraw-Hill.

Margulis, L. and Sagan, D. (2000). *What Is Life*. Berkeley, CA: University of California Press.

Marieb, E & Hoehn, K. (2012). *Human Anatomy and Physiology*. San Francisco: Pearson.

Naydler, J. (1996). *Goethe on Science*. Trowbridge, UK: Cromwell Press.

Nova. (2009). *What Is Evo-Devo?* http://www.pbs.org/wgbh/nova/evolution/what-evo-devo.html

Pelikan, W. (1997). *Healing Plants*. Chestnut Ridge, NY: Mercury Press.

Poppelbaum, H. (2014). *Man and Animal*. UK: Rudolf Steiner Press.

Portmann, A. (1976). *Einfuehrung in die Morphologie der Wirbeltiere*. Basel: Schwabe & Co.

Rohen, J. (2007). *Functional Morphology*. Hillsdale, NY: Adonis.

_____. (2003). *Funktionelle Anatomie des Menschen*. Stuttgart, New York: Schattauer.

_____. (2001). *Funktionelle Anatomie des Nervensystems*. Stuttgart, New York: Schattauer.

Rosslenbroich, B. (2014). *The Origin of Autonomy*. New York: Springer.

Sadler, T. (2000). *Langman's Medical Embryology*. Baltimore: Lippincott, Williams & Wilkins.

Schad, W. (2014). Das Nervensystem und die Uebersinnliche Organization des Menschen. In *Die Doppelnatur des Ich*, W. Schad, Ed. Stuttgart: Freies Geistesleben.

_____. (1986). *Erziehung Ist Kunst*. Frankfurt: Fischer Verlag.

_____. (1977). *Man and Animals*. Garden City, NY: Waldorf Press.

_____. (2012). *Sauegetiere und Mensch*. 2 Bde. Stuttgart: Freies Geistesleben.

Schmidt, R. (1975). *Dynamisch Ernaehrungslehre*. St. Gallen: Proteus Verlag.

Selg, P. (2000). *Vom Logos Menschlicher Physis*. Dornach: Verlag am Goetheanum.

Stanford Encyclopedia of Philosophy (2015). https://plato.stanford.edu/entries/johann-herbart/

Steiner, R. (1919). *Discussions with Teachers*.

_____. (1950). *Goethe the Scientist*. New York: Anthroposophic Press.

_____. (1910). *The Human Soul and the Animal Soul*. Berlin, Nov. 10.

_____. (1917, 2012). *Riddles of the Soul*. UK: Rudolf Steiner Press.

_____. (1886, 1988). *The Science of Knowing*. Spring Valley, NY: Mercury Press.

_____. (1920). *Warmth Course*, Lecture IX. UK: Rudolf Steiner Press.

Suchantke, A. (2009). *Metamorphosis: Evolution in Action*. Hillsdale, NY: Adonis.

_____. (1981. *Menschenkundliche Hinweise*. Erziehungs-kunst, 3/4 1981.

Tortora, G. & Derrickson, B. (2013). *Principles of Anatomy and Physiology*. Hoboken, NJ: John Wiley & Sons.

Van De Graaff, K. & Fox, S. (1998). *Concepts of Human Anatomy and Physiology*. Chicago: W.C. Brown.

Van der Pals, L. (1984). *Was ist Eurythmie?* Dornach: Verlag am Goetheanum.

Verhulst, J. (2003). *Developmental Dynamics in Humans and Other Primates*. Hillsdale, NY: Adonis.

Wehr, G. (2003). *Jung and Steiner. The Birth of a New Psychology*. Great Barrington, MA: SteinerBooks.

Wolff, O. (2014). Nerv und Muskel. Biochemische Grundlagen zum Verständnis ihrer Funktion. In Die *Doppelnatur des Ich*, W. Schad, ed. Stuttgart: Freies Geistesleben.

Commentary: The microcosm and macrocosm

In each part of the body there is an emphasis of one aspect, e.g., the head is mostly head, but there is the feeling part of the head = the nose, and the metabolic-limb part = mouth.

Steiner refers to language teaching, noting that before the age of 7 imitation is the main way to learn, but afterwards we work with the grammatical side of language. When the teacher brings firmness and power into language by creative teaching of grammar, reading and writing, this is like the second teeth but a teething of the soul.

The activity of imagination needs to be permeated with inner warmth as a way of strengthening the soul development from 12th to 15th years—the 6th to 8th grades. The soul capacities that develop during this time need to be permeated with inner love in the imagination. We need to bring imagination into the growing power of judgment in history, geography, geometry and arithmetic.

Rudolf Steiner concludes these lectures with the advice: The teacher must never get sour. There is an inner morality in teaching. The motto: Imbue thyself with the power of imagination, Have courage for the truth, Sharpen your feeling for responsibility of soul.

Study Questions

1. What does it mean to teach with imagination?
2. Why is teaching with imagination important for early adolescents (ages 12–14)?
3. Give an example of presenting the same lesson with and without imaginative content.
4. How is *imagination* different from *fantasy* (English meanings)?
5. Which of the six basic exercises would help you not to grow sour?

When working with *Study of Man* in teacher training, I also ask a few other things of the students:
1. For each lecture, I ask them to note passages that are significant, eye-opening, or made them say "aha"—called exclamation points; those are marked "!"
2. For each lecture, I ask them to note question marks for passages where they wonder about the meaning; those are marked "?"

3. For each, mark passages with –m– that could be fruitful
    subjects for meditation.

Then as we go through the text, they bring up the moments of !
? and –m– as we go.

4. I also ask the students to choose a passage or concept
    from any lecture and represent it artistically. Many fine
    conversations ensue when these are presented.

5. I like to make visual diagrams of various aspects of the
    lectures, and I encourage students to do the same and
    share them.

Artistic Work

The PSC took up the study of Lecture 6 in *Study of Man* in October of 2016. The lecture addresses the study of the threefold human being from the point of view of the spirit, or degrees of consciousness. Specifically, Steiner describes thinking as wakeful, the will as sleeping, and feeling as a dream-like state. In our first artistic session with this lecture, members were invited to use pastels, black and white drawing, or poetry to ponder sleeping and waking. In the second session, the central topic was "dreaming, with suggestions of sleeping and waking on the edges."

What follows are a poem and two examples of black and white drawings. The poem, written by a member who had just given a eulogy for his deceased wife, takes into account the earlier suggestion by Steiner that the will is connected to life after death and thinking-images to life before birth.

She carries fields of spirit in her wake,
Onward to her wake, and to the spirit fields;
He, wakeful, speaks the pictures of her past,
Past youth, past childhood, past first breath.

He fields her past, in images;
She carries his awakened images
In her flow of ripened deeds, in spirit,
Onward to the light.

Sleeping and Waking:

Dreaming:

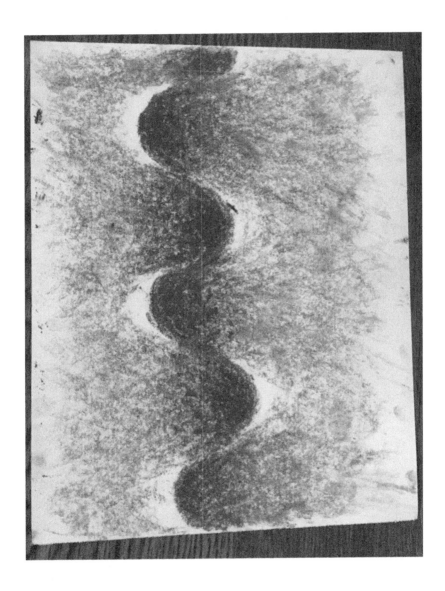

41114379R00089

Made in the USA
Middletown, DE
03 April 2019